Alpine Circus

Alpine Circus

A Skier's Exotic Adventures
at the Snowy Edge of the World

MICHAEL FINKEL

THE LYONS PRESS

First Edition

Printed in Canada

Design and composition by SR Desktop Services, Ridge, NY

10   9   8   7   6   5   4   3   2   1

Library of Congress Cataloging-in-Publication Data

Finkel, Michael.
    Alpine circus : a skier's exotic adventures at the snowy edge of the world / Michael Finkel. — 1st Lyons Press ed.
    p. cm.
  ISBN 1-55821-924-2
    1. Skiers — United States Biography.   2. Downhill skiing.
I. Title.
GV854.2.F56S54   1999
796.93'5'092—dc21
  [B]   99–34525
                                         CIP

Portions of this book have appeared in *Skiing* magazine; "The Other Side of Crazy" appeared in *Snowboard Life.*

Grateful acknowledgement is made to Hank deVré for use of the photograph that appears throughout this book.

To Rick Kahl, for never saying no.

*Great things are done when men
and mountains meet;
This is not done by jostling in the street.*
—WILLIAM BLAKE

Contents

Introduction

S kiing has ruined my life.

Or so I have been told, most pointedly by a pair of people I will identify only by the code names Mom and Dad. It's true, I suppose: My attachment to the sport has dashed any plans I've ever had for a stable or financially secure career. Because of skiing, I have been both ceremoniously and unceremoniously dumped by a liftline's worth of wonderful, marriageable women. For my sport, I have moved to the hinterlands of the Northern Rockies, hundreds of miles from the nearest Starbucks. And, as a result of my cravings, I have produced, at age 30, a set of knees that emits a noise when I flex them rather like someone playing "Chopsticks" on the piano.

None of this is my fault. I was forced to learn to ski when I was five years old, well before the age of rational consent and far too young to have any control over an addictive substance (e.g., powder snow). Who forced me to learn? Why, the pair I mentioned earlier—code names Mom and Dad. And not only did this couple make me learn, they kept dragging me back to the hills, over and over and over again. They even coerced me into submission by repeatedly buying me new and better equipment. What chance did I ever really have of leading a productive life?

College nearly saved me. I went to school in Pennsylvania, where the ski hills were a fine substitute for a 12-step program. Twelve ski trips to the icy purgatory of the Poconos, and I'd broken my addiction. I was set to become a financier. I was prepped for Wall Street. I owned a suit.

And then, during my senior year, I made the mistake of entering an essay contest, one sponsored by none other than *Ski* magazine. The puckish gods of glissade conspired to have me win. My prize was a spring break trip to Breckenridge, Colorado. The snow was soft and deep, and renewed nightly. I was off the wagon.

Upon my return, the magazine asked me to scribble an anecdote or two about my trip. They placed my paragraphs in the magazine. Then they sent me a check—a decent-size one. For writing a story about skiing. I had sipped the Kool-Aid; I had seen the light. Wall Street was abandoned. I wanted to write about skiing.

It was then, at the tender age of 21, that I met Rick Kahl. Rick is the editor-in-chief of *Skiing* magazine. While I was still reeling from my publishing debut, Rick lured me onto his magazine's staff. He made me travel the world, on his dime, seeking out the most unusual and remarkable places to ski, expenses be damned. Then, like feeding junk to a junkie, he paid me a fair salary to write about my experiences. I had hit rock bottom.

Other publications came calling, each with their own dirty needles. *Sports Illustrated, The Atlantic Monthly, The New York Times, Outside.* Because of Rick and others, I have ridden on yak-back into the mountains of central China. I have read anti-American propaganda on the streets of Iran. I have watched sunrise from the summit of Kilimanjaro. I have been bitten by a dog (in Bolivia) and buried in an avalanche (in Montana) and burned on my derrière (in Scotland). I have witnessed the northern lights and run with the Olympic torch and launched myself off a ski jump. I once spent an afternoon skiing down a runaway truck ramp, which provoked a trucker's publication named *Overdrive* to honor me with its "Pothole of the Month" citation. Never let it be said that I am not an award-winning writer.

At this point, beyond any hope of redemption, I am now seeking to introduce the untainted to the dark forces of recreation. In order to do so, I have gathered together the most compelling of my adventures, the ones that have contributed unduly to my life's stunted course. Read them, and I can only hope I'll foster in some small way the ruin of your life, too.

Alpine Circus

In the Land of the Ayatollahs

In addition to state-sponsored misogyny, ill-tempered aya-tollahs, and a death sentence on Salman Rushdie, the Islamic Republic of Iran is home to quite a few ski resorts. I learned of the resorts a couple of years ago, when I came across a photo of one in an old *National Geographic* magazine. I later telephoned the Iranian mission to the United Nations, in New York City. An official there not only confirmed the resorts' existence, he was driven to near poetry—he described majestic peaks in Iran's northern highlands and great quantities of light, dry powder, the moisture sucked out of the snow clouds on the trip across the Iranian desert. He mentioned modern ski resorts, with hotels and gondolas and midmountain restaurants, and said tens of thousands of Iranians were avid skiers, men and women included.

This was a remarkable bit of information. Iran is a country in which most women are forbidden to appear in public without a tentlike chador that conceals all hints of body shape or hair color; where alcohol is prohibited, as is rock music, dancing, jewelry, and anything else deemed un-Islamic by the ayatollahs who run the country; where an Iranian editor whose magazine was shut down by the government said, as quoted in a front-page article in a recent *New York Times,* "There is deep fear and absolutely no freedom of expression." It was impossible to imagine these same Iranians floating blithely down the slopes.

The man from the United Nations swore his descriptions were accurate. I said I'd like to see the ski areas myself. He informed me that, pending a miraculous shift in U.S.-Iran relations, I was not invited to visit the resorts—nor anyplace else in Iran, for that matter.

That pretty much sealed it. I resolved to go.

The United States and Iran have not shared diplomatic relations since the morning of November 4, 1979, when militants seized the American embassy in Tehran, took 52 people hostage, and held them for 444 days. Still, it is not illegal for Americans to visit Iran. Just inadvisable, and difficult. It took me more than a year to obtain a visa. I wrote fawning letters to various Iranian authorities—"I am looking forward to availing myself of the wonderful hospitality of your government"—and masqueraded as a professional skier rather than a magazine writer. (Iranians are skittish about journalists.) I even worked with an Iranian-born travel agent.

Nevertheless, my first visa application was rejected. My second was held up in the Iranian mission for more than a month. Literally hours before my scheduled flight I finally secured a visa for myself and a California-based photographer named Marc Muench. We departed on February 25.

◆ ◆ ◆

Iran's peculiarities began to emerge even before we landed. As the airplane banked toward Tehran International Airport, after the brief flight from Paris, two announcements were broadcast. First, we were told to set our watches two and a half hours ahead of Paris time. Not two hours, not three, but two and a half. Iran, electing not to cooperate with any of its neighbors and most of the world, has established its very own time zone.

Then came the second announcement: "All women must wear Islamic dress before disembarking from the plane." Women reached into handbags and overhead compartments and brought out dark-colored shawls and headscarves. They wiped away makeup and covered their heads. What was once a vivid collection of passengers faded into unsettling anonymity. I didn't see a woman's hairdo for the remainder of my trip.

The travel agent I worked with had arranged a guide and translator, and we were met in the airport lobby by a silver-haired man, a chain-smoker, impeccably dressed in a tan suit and wool sweater. (But not wearing a tie: Ties are seen as symbolic of Western mores, and are therefore unacceptable.) Iran is a formal country; our guide introduced himself as Mr. Atigheh, and that is what we called him. Marc and I insisted it wasn't necessary to use our surnames, so for the entire visit Mr. Atigheh referred to us as Mr. Marc and Mr. Mike.

We'd landed in the middle of the night. Mr. Atigheh dropped us off at the nearby Hotel Esteghlal. Before the Islamic Revolution, in 1979, it had been the Hilton. The glass wall around our room's balcony had three bullet holes in it. On the one channel available on our television, a turbaned man was holding a Koran and chanting verses in Farsi, Iran's primary language.

We were awakened by the sunrise. Our hotel room overlooked Tehran. The city is huge, 14 million people, and is fashioned mostly of concrete, with a jaundiced cloud perpetually hovering above it like a grim portent. To the south, east, and west, Soviet-style tenements spill into a cracked brown desert. To the north, though, the city sprawl is halted by an imposing mountain range, wholly devoid of trees, rising in a dozen sharp-ridged waves—dun-colored near the city, darker farther back, and then, against the horizon, gleaming white with snow. These are the Elburz Mountains, a volcanic chain bridging the lowlands along the Caspian Sea and the vast, dry central plateau. It is home to most of Iran's ski areas.

Mr. Atigheh eventually arrived, and we departed for the mountains. The route took us through Tehran. Upon my request, we drove past the former American embassy. It is now called the U.S. Espionage Den—the new name is advertised, in Farsi and English, on the front gate—and is used to train Islamic Revolutionary Guards, Iran's version of the KGB. Nearby was a five-story-high mural depicting an American flag. In place of the stars was a field of skulls, and written across the flag, in giant letters, in English, it read: DOWN WITH THE USA.

"If anyone asks where you're from," said Mr. Atigheh, "be sure to tell them Canada."

♦ ♦ ♦

Iran's ski areas were built in the early 1970s, when the final Shah, Mohammed Reza Pahlavi, still ruled. Buoyed by billions of dollars in oil revenues, the Shah had attempted to westernize Iran. He gave women the right to vote and doubled the literacy rate. He allied his nation with the United States, courted the Coca-Cola Company, permitted McDonald's restaurants to open—and developed ski resorts. Pahlavi himself became an avid skier, and Iranian ski racers competed in the 1972 and 1976 Olympic Games. But the Shah's autocratic leadership style and his extensive use of the secret police led to popular unrest. Devout Muslims wanted reforms scaled back. The general populace was angry that only a tiny minority profited from oil sales. On January 16, 1979, Pahlavi was overthrown.

Ayatollah Ruhollah Khomeini ascended to power and established a clergy-controlled Islamic theocracy. (There is an elected president, but he is subservient to the many ayatollahs.) Western influences were eliminated—no more Big Macs. Non-Persian music was banned. A person could be arrested for carrying a guitar. Women were forced to wear the chador; the U.S. hostages were seized; and thousands of dissenters were executed. The ski areas, emblematic of the depraved and amoral Western world, were shut down. For liberalized Iranians, dark ages had descended.

But then something curious happened. Skiing might be depraved and amoral, but several high-ranking ayatollahs were quite keen on it. Hundreds of other Iranian skiers, risking punishment, voiced their displeasure with the ban. And in one of the few cases in the past 20 years in which popular demand has triumphed over Islamic decrees, the areas reopened for business three winters after they shut down.

Iran is a large country, nearly the size of Alaska. Its topography is roughly soup-bowl shaped: a central desert hemmed by mountain ranges—the Zagros, the Kopet-Dag, the Elburz—all of which receive significant snowfall. Nobody I spoke with, including the director of Iranian skiing, would tell me how many ski areas the country has. No phone book has been printed since the Revolution, and any type of information, no matter how innocuous, is guarded by the Iranian government like a state secret. My guess is 10 areas. There are five well-known resorts clustered in the mountains near Tehran, and a good estimate, culled from various brochures and pre-Revolution guidebooks, is another five scattered throughout the other ranges.

Marc and I were headed to Dizin, undoubtedly the largest and most sophisticated of the ski hills, 75 miles north of Tehran. It was Thursday afternoon, the start of the Iranian weekend. (Friday is the Muslim Sabbath.) The narrow road out of Tehran was crowded with lead-footed skiers racing their Iranian-made Pecans—they look like little Peugeots— away from the city. I saw modern, top-of-the-line skis, and even a few snowboards, but nobody seemed to own a ski rack. The acceptable Iranian gear-transportation method is to stick the skis almost straight up, like a collection of antennas, through the rolled-down passenger-side window, the tails pinched between the inside of the door and the front seat.

We followed the Chalus River upstream, into the mountains. For a few miles, there were tight stands of cottonwood and sycamore, but the vegetation soon faded, replaced by intricate sandstone formations. We passed dozens of little teahouses, each with three or four tables and a brass teapot resting on a wood-burning stove. Snow lined the road. A pair of apple sellers rubbed their hands over a roadside campfire. On the surrounding hills we could see ruins of ancient stone houses. Here and there, painted on buildings and billboards, were portraits of Iranian soldiers—bearded, sharp-eyed—who had been martyred in the eight-year war against Iraq. Women walking along the road seemed scarcely more than shadows, swathed head to toe in ebony chadors, one end of the fabric clenched between their teeth to conceal their mouths.

The road ended at the ski hill. We passed under a stone archway and into a gravel parking lot. The lifts were just shutting down for the day, and skiers were streaming off the mountain. Dizin is big. Three gondolas and a handful of other lifts link a half dozen high-alpine bowls, all of them rippled with hillocks and crags and webs of rambling streambeds. There is not a single tree. According to statistics printed on the trail map, Dizin receives an average of 22 feet of snow each winter. The summit elevation is 11,360 feet; the vertical drop is nearly 3,000 feet. It's the type of place you can ski for a month and never ride the same fall line twice.

The base area, though, was sparse. There was one run-down-looking hotel, and that is where we stayed. It was a typical Iranian flimflam: $25 a night for Iranian citizens, $100 for foreigners. When the man at the front desk demanded some identification, we handed over our passports. This caused somewhat of a commotion—the desk clerk seemed neither thrilled nor upset, just disconcerted. Evidently, Marc and I were only the second group of Americans to visit Dizin since the Revolution. The mountain manager, a man named Mokhtar Seiyd, was summoned from his office to meet us.

I liked Mokhtar immediately. He had rich, mocha skin and a demeanor so gentle it felt subversive, a deliberate counterpoint to the prevailing harshness. He was one of the few Iranian men I met who didn't have a mustache. Mokhtar was also as close as an Iranian can get to being a ski bum: He was 38 years old and had been working at Dizin for 17 years. His English was excellent. When we talked, there was a degree of openness—a willingness to sidestep the propagandist line—that was missing from my conversations with Mr. Atigheh. I called him by his first name. And Mokhtar was unique among Iranians I spoke with in his ability to tell ribald jokes.

We toured the base area. In addition to the hotel, Dizin contains seven small rental shops and an enormous police station. This station is a branch office for a widely feared segment of the Islamic Revolutionary Guards called the Komite, which specializes in punishing religious transgressors. The soldiers live uphill of the hotel in a lavish mansion that was originally built as a palace for the Shah. Their uniforms contain a patch depicting a bloody hand clutching a rifle.

The presence of skiing, it turns out, is still a contentious issue in Iran. Hard-line ayatollahs don't like the sport: It promotes impure mingling of the sexes. The Komite doesn't like it: Skiers have a history of disregarding authority. Dizin's reputation as a place of rampant blasphemy has earned it the nickname Sin Mountain—a name, Mokhtar told me, that the skiers themselves take pride in. This angers the Komite. When the mood strikes, soldiers descend upon the

9

mountain and harass skiers. But the soldiers' power is limited. Several high-ranking Iranian officials ski Dizin, as do the few remaining avant-garde ayatollahs. (They aren't very good, admitted Mokhtar.) The resort, despite some powerful opposition, continues to operate, with some 200,000 Iranian skiers coming for a visit each winter.

◆ ◆ ◆

Breakfast the next morning, in the hotel lobby, was mobbed. Bread was being baked in an igloo-shaped oven in the rear of the restaurant—flat loaves, about the thickness of a pizza, as soft and delicious as fresh tortillas. They were served with honey, goat cheese, and tea.

Lift tickets (same price no matter the nationality) cost 16,000 rials—about five dollars. On the front of the ticket was a photo of Alberto Tomba. The short walk to the nearest gondola took me past a small, whitewashed mosque, a new Pisten Bully grooming machine, six Iranian flags, and a billboard with a scary portrait of Ayatollah Ali Khamenei, the religious leader who replaced Khomeini after his death in 1989. The air was warm and windless.

Marc and I boarded the four-person gondola and were joined by a pair of Iranian men. They looked to be in their early 30s; one spoke a little English. He said his name was Reza, which is what half of Iranian men seemed to be named. This was Reza's first day on a new pair of Salomons, his first new pair of skis in five years, and he told me he hadn't been able to sleep he was so anxious to try them.

That's normal, I said. "If the weather is nice tomorrow," added Reza, "I will skip work and ski more." That's even more normal, I said. At midmountain we passed over a restaurant. Reza mentioned that it was the local pizza place. Of course, I said. Ski areas are ski areas. For the first time since I'd landed in Iran, I was beginning to feel relaxed.

Then I stepped out of the gondola and headed to the top terminal's exit. "No!" shouted Reza. "That's the women's exit, to the women's slope."

It took me all day to figure out the rules of Iranian skiing. One of the main difficulties was that the skiing rules, like many rules in Iran, were subject to immediate change without warning. When the Komite soldiers were out, for example, the rules were completely different than when they were hanging around their palace. "Normal here," said one of the few non-Iranian skiers I met, an official with the Canadian embassy, "is having absolutely no clue what's normal."

Generally, though, the rules went like this: Men and women cannot ride the lifts together. For lifts that begin at the bottom of the mountain, where the Komite is most likely to be watching, men and women must also wait on separate lift lines. For upper-mountain lifts, there is one line but still segregated ridership. An exception is married couples, who may ride together provided they are prepared to show a valid marriage certificate upon demand from a Revolutionary Guard. Women must ski with their heads completely covered—a ski hat won't do. And if a woman's jacket doesn't descend below her knees, she must wear a black skirt over her ski pants to cover the offensive parts. Men can wear whatever they want. (I'm not sure how women felt about this: Islamic law forbids a woman from speaking casually to men other than her husband or relatives, so I didn't talk with any Iranian women.) Ostensibly, men and women must also stick to different sides of the slopes—Dizin's main runs are divided by wooden fences—but unless a large number of soldiers were present this stipulation was roundly ignored. None of this stopped women from skiing; surprisingly, there were nearly as many female skiers as male.

At the top of the gondola, before Marc and I had taken even one run, Mokhtar appeared—he seemed to be keeping an eye on us—and insisted we meet the Dizin ski patrol. He took us to the patrol shack, an aluminum-sided hut the size of a garden shed. Inside were nine patrollers, all men, all nattily dressed in light-blue one-piece ski suits. They were crammed around a table eating flatbread and drinking tea. They jumped up and introduced themselves—Reza and Reza and Mehdi and Said and Abdhul and Nejat and Amir and Moshen and Jabar. Three more cups were produced, and Mokhtar, Marc, and I squeezed in. The door was shut. None of the patrollers spoke much English, but we took turns smiling awkwardly at one another and clinking glasses. Then we downed the tea and hurried out, primed for skiing.

The dozen of us flew down the mountain. A few inches of snow had fallen the day before we arrived, and it was still untracked. Most Iranians are beginning or lower-intermediate skiers, and they tend to stick solely to groomed runs. We hit the fresh snow, which was already turning to corn beneath the blinding sun. The patrollers were excellent skiers, fast and wiggly—a late-'70s sort of style—and we descended side by side across the whole of one bowl, all of us whooping loudly. A whoop's a whoop, Farsi or English. I tumbled once, a complete somersault, and popped up coated with snow. Mehdi taught me a Farsi phrase: *poudr b'zork*—powder pig.

At the bottom the patrollers left to patrol, but Mokhtar stayed with us to ski. Or, rather, to drink tea. Tea drinking is Iran's national pastime. Before skiing again, we stepped into the gondola operators' shack and had another cup, while drying our gloves on an old kerosene heater. Mokhtar showed me the proper Iranian way to use sugar: clench a cube between the front teeth and allow the tea to filter through. Then we took a run. Then we rested at a warming hut and drank a cup of tea. Then a run. Then we stopped at a wooden table set up aside one slope, where a man was grilling lamb kabobs over a hibachi, and drank a cup of tea. Then another run. And then time for tea at the midmountain lodge. With the exception of a small group of expert skiers, everyone on the mountain seemed to be doing this. For most Iranians, skiing apparently serves only to separate tea breaks.

The two-story midmountain lodge is the big place to hang out at Dizin. The lower level, clouded with cigarette smoke, is reserved for men; the upper level is for women and their husbands. But the real scene was out front, where both men and women could rent beach chairs and sun themselves. Persian music was playing through a set of loudspeakers. (Persian music, which has a strong resemblance to John Tesh compositions, is acceptable. Rock and roll, or any type of music with a catchy beat, is out.) Everyone was drinking either tea or Zam Zam soda, which is manufactured at a pre-Revolution Coca-Cola plant.

Two Komite soldiers, wearing khaki pants and black jackboots, roamed about, but they did not seem to mind that there was obvious intersex mingling going on. I asked Mokhtar why the guards were there.

"Today, making sure all the women stay covered. Tomorrow—who knows?"

The thing I found most puzzling about the scene, however, had nothing to do with the guards. It was the ski jackets. American football, basketball, and baseball teams were advertised on the back of a startling number of parkas. In a two-minute span I spotted jackets promoting the New York Yankees, the Oakland Raiders, the Georgetown Hoyas, the Kansas City Chiefs, and something called the Chicago Giants. Even Mokhtar's hat displayed the black-and-red logo of the Chicago Bulls.

That's not all. The lodge sold Winston cigarettes and Twix candy bars, both with MADE IN THE USA printed on every package. In the hotel basement the evening before, a group of people had gathered to watch a Farsi-dubbed version of *Star*

Wars. On the drive up, I'd seen Mickey Mouse grinning from a billboard advertisement. Of the few strangers to whom I'd admitted my true nationality, not one had a single ill word to say about America. Instead, they peppered me with endless questions about basketball, and *Baywatch,* and Bill Clinton. Several wanted to know if I could sell them music. One man told me he would pay absolutely anything for a Whitney Houston cassette.

At the same time, the Iranian government regularly refers to the United States as the "Great Satan" and frequently issues proclamations denouncing its cultural exports. According to Mr. Atigheh, the punishment for simply carrying U.S. currency, which Marc and I both had, can be jail time. (Mr. Atigheh paid for everything in rials; we paid him dollars in private.)

"The Komite have no idea what's written on people's jackets," Mokhtar told me. "And many people, educated people, really like America. Skiers here are mostly educated people." But the explanation did little to settle my confusion. It was a typical Iranian paradox.

♦ ♦ ♦

Near the end of the day, I rode a double chair with a young medical student named Mehryar. He complained about the absence of bars and discos in Iran, and said he could not receive a tourist visa to visit any countries other than Libya and Algeria. "But when I am skiing," he told me, "I am as free as anyone anywhere—as free as you."

I was moved by Mehryar's sentiments, but my lift-mate was mistaken. When I came down from the hill, Mr. Atigheh, who had been milling around the base area all day, casually mentioned that he'd seen the Revolutionary Guards arrest several skiers: a group of seven young men and women, unmarried and unrelated to one another, who'd made the mistake of sitting together in the hotel restaurant, and a handful of women who had improperly covered their hair. (A single visible strand is enough to warrant punishment.) Apparently, the guards at the base area were not as lax as the ones at midmountain.

I asked what would happen to the skiers. "Oh, they were probably lectured for a few hours and then sent back to Tehran," said Mr. Atigheh. But after a little prodding, he admitted that this was just a guess. "Nobody really knows," he said. If any were repeat offenders, a public whipping was possible, and maybe jail time. Iran is no place in which to be entangled with the law. Thieves can be sentenced to amputation of fingers. Drug dealers are executed. Public floggings are commonplace. And while it is legal for a man to have as many as four wives, if a married woman is caught sleeping with another man, both are tied together and stoned to death.

Neither Mokhtar nor Mr. Atigheh appeared the least bit troubled by the arrests. Apparently, such actions are an everyday occurrence. If anything, though, my hosts' indifference seemed cause for greater alarm. Since I didn't understand Iranian laws, how was I to know if I were breaking one?

Mokhtar sensed my anxiety and insisted I put the incidents out of my mind. "Let's have some fun," he said. He suggested we drive down the road to the first village and eat a traditional Iranian dinner.

♦ ♦ ♦

We went to a nameless restaurant that had been converted from a one-car garage. Mokhtar ordered a dish called *dizi*. Dizi is a type of stew made from cubes of lamb and assorted beans. Each bowl comes with its own pestle, and before you eat you must spend several minutes mashing the stew into souplike consistency. Then you slurp it down. Iranians eat extraordinarily fast and, save for the slurping, in complete silence. Dizi is the Iranian surrogate for a burrito: cheap, filling, and good. The meal cost the equivalent of $1.25 each.

Afterward we stopped at a teahouse. The importance of teahouses in Iran cannot be overestimated. They are the Iranian substitute for bars. At least for men; no women are allowed. Mokhtar requested a round of tea and a *ghalyan*—a water pipe. Out came the most magnificent hookah I have ever seen: three feet high, made of ceramic and wood, and decorated with miniature portraits of ancient Persian kings. A long, red tube emerged from the bottom of the pipe.

A teahouse worker filled a cup with coals, lit them with a match, and walked out of the shop. I followed him out. The man attached the cup to a thin chain and spun the coals, creating a circular orange contrail in front of him, like a fire dancer. When all the coals were glowing he walked back inside and set the cup atop the pipe. We began to smoke. Mokhtar and Mr. Atigheh took long, soulful drags, held in the smoke, then let it go in slow, dignified exhalations. The ghalyan bubbled peacefully. We passed around the pipe. The tobacco was smooth and delicious, as potent as beer. It made me feel as though I were floating. There were two other tables in the café, one with a group of uniformed traffic cops, the other with a trio of locals. We all smoked, a pipe at each table. When the tobacco was finished one of the locals, a fat man with a ruddy face, burst into song—a Persian folk song, Mokhtar told me. We ordered another round of tobacco and smoked it. "I'm drunk," said Mr. Atigheh. It was almost eight o'clock—a late night by Iranian standards. Within minutes, the place cleared out. I was asleep by nine.

◆ ◆ ◆

Saturday is an Iranian workday, so the ski area was nearly empty the next morning. At breakfast I watched the lift workers—old men, wearing wool blazers and rubber boots— come into the restaurant and stand in line, waiting for their stack of bread. All day they load lifts and pick at the bread.

Once again, Marc and I began the morning in the patrol shack. After we finished our tea, one of the patrollers produced a small bongo drum and began pounding out a beat. We clapped in unison, and the patroller began to sing. More folk music. Then the drum was passed over to Marc. He started thumping, and everybody looked at him to sing, but he shook his head and pointed across the shack at me.

Everybody looked my way, still clapping, and the only thing that popped into my head was an old army marching chant I'd learned from my father. So I sang it. After a few verses every patroller was shouting out the refrain—"Left! Left! Left-right-left!"—and I sang until we dissolved into laughter and spilled out of the shack, wired and giddy, and noticed that a crowd had gathered around, wondering what the hell had been going on inside. We ignored the crowd and clicked into our skis and took a full-speed run beneath a blue blazing sky.

Afterward, I skied a few laps alone, stopping often and looking out over the whole of the Elburz range, the horizon dominated by the perfect cone of Mount Damavand, nearly 19,000 feet high. I deposited my spare change in one of the metal boxes that are posted at the top of each lift, for donations to the poor. Just before noon I stopped in the base area, near the mosque, and watched two women sled down a small hill, their chadors billowing behind them. It was a relaxed day. Even the two Revolutionary Guards patrolling the base area seemed laid back. After the women sledded, the guards walked up the same hill and slid down in their boots.

Soon came the call to prayer. Muslims are obligated to pray five times a day, and the prayer call, echoed from every mosque throughout the Islamic world, is a plaintive, hypnotic hymn, joyous and sad at the same time. People removed their ski boots and filed into the mosque, men in one door, women in another, and the area was almost deserted. I took another run.

Late in the afternoon, Marc and Mokhtar and I met up at the midmountain lodge. For Marc and me, our time in Dizin was nearing an end. Our visas permitted us to remain in Iran only a limited number of days. The weather, though, was too nice to rush, so we rented beach chairs and waited for the patrollers to finish their work. By the time they all showed up, the sun was ready to set. It was the time of day photographers call the magic hour. We skied our last run together as we'd skied our previous runs together—fast and nonstop, with unencumbered joy. We said good-bye in traditional Iranian man-to-man fashion, a kiss on each cheek, and then said good-bye again with a round of good old American high-fives. Mokhtar presented Marc and me each with a hand-sewn prayer mat.

Then we left. On the drive back to Tehran I replayed the visit over and over in my mind. Despite the restrictions imposed on them, the vast majority of skiers at Dizin had easily avoided any troubles—in fact, they had seemed to enjoy a relaxing weekend. Watching them instilled in me a renewed sense of the escapist pleasure, of the simple, powerful autonomy that skiing can provide.

But I couldn't help worrying about the future of Iranian skiing. The most recent crop of ayatollahs, people had told me, are even more intolerantly fundamentalist than any before. They've already banned women from riding motorcycles, and horses, and bicycles. Satellite dishes have recently been prohibited; helicopters fly over Tehran looking for ones that have been smuggled in. Playing cards are now illegal, as is backgammon. Not one of the 1,500 novels submitted to the censors last year was approved for publication. College professors suspected of being disloyal to the government have been beaten. A move is under way to outlaw the Internet.

Recently, however, after an extraordinary presidential election in which the candidate endorsed by most ayatollahs was defeated, a new Iranian president, Mohammed Khatami, was inaugurated. Though he is regarded as a moderate, he must still answer to Iran's inflexible religious leaders. Even so, it is possible that the new president will be able to prevent further erosion of liberties. Perhaps he may even institute reform. I'd been told over and over during my trip that nothing ever happens as expected in Iran.

Still, my conclusion was inescapable. Iranian skiers have been extremely fortunate that their sport has remained out of the ayatollahs' crosshairs. This good fortune can't last forever. One day—it could be tomorrow—skiing will no longer be allowed in Iran.

High Times at Chacaltaya

I have been told that if you can't say something nice, you shouldn't say anything at all. Clearly, the person who told me this has never had to write an essay about skiing at Chacaltaya. Still, I will start with something nice: Chacaltaya is the best ski area in Bolivia. A less polite person might add that it is the only ski area in Bolivia.

I went to Chacaltaya a few seasons ago, in December. I'd read something about the area in a South American guidebook, and curiosity got the better of me. I also persuaded my girlfriend to come with me. At the end of the trip, miraculously, she was still my girlfriend. You might think that South American skiing would take place during the South American winter—June, July, and August. With every other South

American ski hill, you'd be right. But because the access road is impassable during winter months, you can only ski Chacaltaya when you'll be missing fine conditions back home.

The trip to Chacaltaya starts in downtown La Paz, Bolivia's biggest city. Let me tell you about La Paz. Have you ever wondered what it would look like if you dug up an entire American metropolis—say, L.A.—and dumped the whole caboodle into the Grand Canyon? If so, you should check out La Paz. That's precisely what it looks like, except no McDonald's. Also, the water is polluted, the air tastes like the inside of your shoe, and about every tenth of a second a bus comes a millimeter from running you over. Otherwise, it's quite a nice city.

You sign up for the ski trip at a place called Club Andino Boliviano, which looks like a back-alley Off Track Betting joint. The ski area is only open on weekends. I went on a Saturday. A man named Carlos—a very nice man, by the way—picked us up at the club in his Toyota Land Cruiser. There were seven passengers in all: three from Germany, one from Denmark, one from Scotland, and my girlfriend and I. Carlos was the only Bolivian. He said he was a skier, but he wasn't going to ski Chacaltaya.

In spots, the road to Chacaltaya is nice. Mostly, though, the road is a cesspool of mud the width of a large dog, with no guardrail and a drop-off that would allow me to write my last will and testament before we hit bottom. The city of La Paz is 12,000 feet above sea level, and the road only goes up from there. It switchbacks through the ramshackle outdoor markets of the La Paz suburbs—a coca-leaf stand, a papaya-fruit table, a wooden-flute maker, a toilet-bowl dealer. Up onto the treeless altiplano, past clusters of mud-brick houses and small herds of llamas and alpacas. Up and up, higher than the summit of Breckenridge, higher than the summit of Rainier, higher than any point in the contiguous United States, until the glaciated peaks of the Cordillera Real captured us in their shadows.

At 15,600 feet above sea level, according to my wrist-watch's altimeter, we stopped. A man, a woman, and a boy were standing by the side of the road. The woman, like many Bolivian women, was dressed in traditional Chola garb—a colorful, billowy skirt; several layers of pastel petticoats; a woolen shawl; and a brown bowler. It was as if Gauguin, Cézanne, and Magritte had gotten together and selected her wardrobe. She squeezed into the front seat; the other two hopped onto the Toyota's luggage rack. Carlos explained that this was the family that operates the ski-area snack bar. We continued up. It began to hail.

Chacaltaya's base elevation is 17,130 feet. It is, by far, the highest ski area in the world, which means that everyone who goes there suffers from a splitting headache the entire time. It is also the most equatorial ski area in the world, and it contains the world's highest restaurant. Even so, I'm glad I'm not the area's marketing director. There is one run, on an ice-rink-shaped glacier, serviced by a contraption that I will graciously call a lift. The area was founded in 1938 by a man named Raúl Posnasky. Soon after, Raúl died on his own hill in an avalanche. Nobody has volunteered to build any-thing else—Bolivians are a fairly superstitious people—so the place is almost exactly as it was six decades ago. Despite this, Carlos told me, a small but dedicated band of Bolivian skiers does exist, though none showed up the day I visited. There was even a five-man Bolivian ski contingent at the 1988 Calgary Olympics. They fared about as well as the Jamaican bobsled team, but nobody made a movie about the Bolivians.

The base area consists of two buildings: one decrepit and one a little worse. The decrepit one is built of stone, with a corrugated fiberglass roof. Most walk-in freezers are warmer. The snack-bar family served us coca *mate*—tea with coca leaves—which is supposed to help alleviate the effects of alti-tude sickness. It did not. I felt as though several very small people were operating power tools just behind my eyeballs.

The other building—more of a barn, really—houses the engine for the thing I am graciously calling a lift. Whoever built this structure has a weird sense of humor: It is situated on the absolute edge of a thousand-foot cliff. The barn is made of wood and looks as if it has seen one too many windy days. The thing is tilted Tower of Pisa style, leaning out over the cliff. I kept thinking, *Next big gust and that sucker is sliding right off the lip.*

Still, I went inside. Suspended over a tree stump and a wooden dolly is the rusted-out chassis of an ancient tractor.

The engine, a straight six, and the grille and the stick shift are still in place, but all the seats and wheels have been removed. One tire rim, though, is still attached. A half-inch-thick cable, frayed like an old toothbrush, runs in one window of the hut, wraps once around the rim, and exits out another window. From there, the cable plunges down the thousand-foot cliff, extends to the bottom of the glacier, winds around some other tire rims mounted to wooden posts, slithers at ground level up the face of the glacier, winds around more rims, ascends the thousand-foot cliff, and comes back into the barn. Don't worry if you don't understand—even if you did, it'd make no sense. I watched a man take the battery from the car we drove up in and clip it into place on the chassis. He tapped two wires together, and the thing clattered to life, coughing little geysers of gasoline. The man pulled the choke, revved the engine, stuck it in third gear, and lit a cigarette. The rim spun. The cable sped through the hut at an astonishing speed.

To rent ski equipment, I went back to the first building, where a half dozen stray dogs and a few carloads of Bolivian sightseers had gathered. Chacaltaya has 12 sets of rental gear, most of which would be instantly thrown out in the United States. I managed to find a pair of Raichle boots that were only a size and a half too big and contained about two thirds of their intended buckles. My skis were fine, except for a four-inch section on the back of one of them, where the base and topskin had gone separate ways. It looked as though the ski had grown a tail fin. I adjusted the bindings—mid '70s Tyrolias—myself. The poles I selected could've composed the first and last letters of an S.O.S. sign. I think I got the best setup available. It cost me $15 in bolivianos, including use of the lift.

Instead of a lift ticket, at Chacaltaya you are given a piece of the lift. This contraption consists of a short section of rebar with a U-shaped bend at one end and a four-foot length of rope attached to the other. At the end of the rope is a block of wood. Carlos showed me how to wear the thinga-majig around my waist as I skied.

The base buildings are about halfway up the slope, so we began the ski day by walking out onto the glacier and skiing down to the bottom of the lift. The conditions were some-what less than perfect: balls of ice atop a sheet of ice. And where there wasn't ice, at the edge of the glacier, there was a nice layer of black dirt. The six of us who rented ski gear skidded and battled our way down. Given the condition of our equipment, it might've been safer to sled.

Then it was time to load the lift. The man who started the lift slid down the glacier in his black loafers to show us what to do. The way it's supposed to work is you get out your piece of lift, position the U-shaped bend in the rebar so that the cable zips through it, and put the rope between your legs so the block is under your butt poma-style. When you're ready to dislocate your shoulder, you yank back on the rebar, which kinks the cable and locks it in and launches you violently up the slope. Fun. To say it was the worst lift ride of my life is just about as nice as I could ever put it. I was dragged and jerked and slung about like a cat's toy. The block of wood deposited a splinter in my rear. My gloves were shredded. I fell and had to reload seven times.

At least I made it to the top. One poor skier, a German guy, lost a ski on the ride up. The ski did not have a ski brake, and it shot out across the glacier. This man spent the entire day retrieving his ski. By the time he returned, the lift was shut down.

There was better snow on the upper part of the run. I could say it was powder, but I'd be lying. Let's just be nice and call it snow. The sun came out, and it was warm, and the views of La Paz were nice, real nice. I skied three runs, and got no better at riding the lift or coping with the altitude, so I called it a day and went into the stone building to eat. The only thing Chacaltaya has perfectly copied from U.S. resorts is base-lodge food. It is astronomically overpriced and all but inedible. I ordered a meat sandwich, and after one bite I fed it to the stray dogs, whose presence no longer seemed so confounding.

Soon it was time to go. Carlos drove us down the mud slick, back to La Paz. He dropped us off in front of our hotel, and I paid him for the ride. He asked me, in Spanish, what I thought of his country's ski hill. He had a big, proud smile on his face. What could I do? I told him it was nice.

Birth of a Ski Nation

This is what the General Secretary of the Chinese Ski Association said to me: "We will teach as many of the masses to ski as possible. From the masses we will pick the future stars. We will have a strong national team. We will train. And then the champion of the Olympic downhill race will be Chinese. It is the dream of my entire life."

The General Secretary, whose name is Shan Zhaojian, is the most important skier in China. He is a tiny man, thin as a coin, with cab-door ears and an unruly mess of ink-black hair. In 1957, he was the winner of China's first-ever ski race. The race was held on what was then the only ski hill in the country, a place that had been established by Japanese troops during their World War II occupation of northern

China. The hill had been hastily abandoned, equipment and all, after Japan's surrender, and from the detritus of war China had inherited a new sport.

Mr. Shan wore a pink ski jacket over a gray sweater and shiny gray slacks. He spoke quietly, at times almost bashfully, but always with an undercurrent of fierce patriotism. He is well aware that China is poised to become the world's dominant economic power, and by his way of thinking, this domination will soon extend to skiing.

I met with Mr. Shan in a pallid hotel room at the Yabuli Skiing Resort, in the rounded hills of northeastern China, the same region that Japan had overrun 60 years before. Mr. Shan had arrived from Beijing, 500 miles to the south, to observe the unveiling of the first Chinese-made snowgun. I was in China to witness the birth of a ski nation.

Yabuli, as with every ski hill in China, is operated by the government; in China, private land ownership is not permitted. There are five modern ski areas in the nation, all of them in the northeast, where most of the population resides. Yabuli was the first to be built—it opened in 1980—and is the only one large enough to be called a resort. As with the United States, though, the population does not reside where the snowiest mountains are. I had arrived in early March, and already there was no snow. Only one of Yabuli's 15 lifts was in operation; the sole open run was a pitiful muddle of ice patches and dirt streaks and scattered hay.

Mr. Shan is in charge of distributing the country's skiing budget. When we met, his budget was about nil. In a manner that struck me as typically Chinese, the country had decided to leapfrog the usual ski-nation progression. Instead of developing a series of modest local hills that would foster a natural sense of ski culture, the Chinese began by constructing a sprawling "firstly-selected skiing and vacationing resort" (this from the brochure) that not only depleted the national ski budget but, in combination with a Chinese predilection for ignoring most foreign advice, also resulted in a place with an ill-thought-out lift system, with trails cut counter to the fall line, in a province that often receives very little snow. Now, in an attempt to amend Yabuli's most pressing problem, the government was spending all remaining ski-allocated funds to manufacture powerful, jet-engine-type snowguns.

What happened, I wondered, to step one of the General Secretary's dream? By Mr. Shan's estimation, only a couple of thousand Chinese have ever tried skiing. It is difficult to find champions before there are beginners.

"We have problems," Mr. Shan admitted, suddenly humble. "We are still a developing country." He spoke in Mandarin, which was translated by one of my two travel partners, an American named Kyle Westguard. Kyle has spent most of the last 10 years in China, and is, at age 29, the president and CEO of China Ski, a company that is attempting to inject U.S. knowledge into future Chinese ski-area projects—

a delicate task, given China's reluctance to accept foreign guidance. I was also traveling with another precocious global adventurer, Colorado-based photographer Chris Anderson.

Mr. Shan said there were plans to open dozens of small hills throughout the country, and that one day there are sure to be tens of millions of Chinese skiers, but for now, with a tight budget, all he can do is ship equipment to the mountains.

I asked him what he meant by shipping equipment to the mountains.

"In an act of friendship," he said, "the government of Japan has donated used ski gear to the Chinese Ski Association. I have sent the gear to Xinjiang."

Of China's 22 provinces and five autonomous regions, Xinjiang is easily the most remote. It is in the northwest corner of the country, more than 2,000 miles from Beijing, encompassing a vast high-alpine territory bridging the area between Mongolia and Kazakhstan. It is the Chinese equivalent of Siberia.

"Did you have lifts built there too?" I asked. Kyle translated.

"No, only equipment."

"Instructors?"

"No, only equipment. There is snow there, and mountains. They will learn to ski."

Mr. Shan said that he had never been to Xinjiang, but he knew the mountains were big and the snow was abundant. He also told me that there is evidence the region may have been home to the world's first skiers, a designation usually staked by the Norwegians. Mr. Shan claimed, though, that the earliest known written history of skiing is from Xinjiang. People there, he said, were writing about skiing 2,500 years ago. It was clear that he expected this area to be his farmgrounds for future champions.

When we finished our meeting, after a long round of good-byes, Kyle, Chris, and I knew precisely where we were headed.

◆ ◆ ◆

The largest city in Xinjiang is called Urumchi. It is close to nothing. To get there by train from eastern China requires 76 hours of travel. An airplane takes only four hours, but China's domestic flights have a reputation for unexpectedly tumbling out of the sky. Nonetheless, we elected to take the plane. Kyle made the arrangements, and upon phoning Urumchi's government-run travel service, was able to locate a guide who said he was an avid skier, and, in the event the plane made it that far, would gladly meet us at the airport.

We flew west from Beijing. From the airplane window the landscape looked like an endless succession of brick-colored dunes. Where there was wind, the sands of the Gobi Desert swirled and gathered in cigar-smoke forms. Now and again, at an oasis, I saw signs of human life—tents, cattle—but there were no cities. Despite its population, China is predominantly rural. One in five people in the world is Chinese;

35

one in seven is a Chinese peasant. Away from the metropolises of the east coast, the nation is exceedingly poor. In fertile areas, the fields are plowed by horses; on most roads, donkey carts outnumber cars. The average per-capita income is less than $50 per year. Several million people still live in caves.

Shortly before we landed (on the runway, without incident), the geography abruptly shifted. We flew over the Tianshan Mountains—the Heavenly Mountains—which rise to nearly 18,000 feet. They are broad and white and majestic, like an assemblage of Rainiers, only with steepled summits and a distinctly unheavenly sense about them of quiet menace. Geologically speaking, they are young peaks, and still growing.

Our guide was an effusive 25-year-old named Liu Yu Ling, who was at the airport with a driver and minivan. He asked us to call him Philippe. His new girlfriend, he said, speaks French, which had evidently prompted him to become an instant Francophile. Philippe is pudgy, which is rare for a Chinese, and extroverted, which is even rarer, and he possessed the sort of manic grinning energy that I associate with many of my closest ski-bum friends. He spoke only two phrases of English, one of which he utilized as a greeting, shouting across the airport lobby as he saw us coming, ski bags balanced over our shoulders: "I like ski! I like ski!" I knew straight off he'd be an excellent addition to the group.

Urumchi is an ugly city. The skyline is smokestacks and blocky tenement-style buildings and the air is acrid with the smell of burning coal. There are no trees. But along its wide avenues there is also the buzzy, reckless feel of a true frontier land. Urumchi is home to a wild mix of ethnic groups, which is an extreme oddity in China, where 95 percent of the people (including Philippe) are Han Chinese. Here, though, there are significant populations of Uighurs, Uzbeks, Tazhiks, Mongols, Tatars, and Kazakhs. The market sells dried snakes and powdered rams' horns and bejeweled knives and an expressive style of headwear in which the pom-pom *is* the hat. This is actually worn on the streets, and makes the wearer appear as though he has recently put his tongue in a light socket. We could not resist purchasing a few. The price was totaled on an abacus.

Philippe took us out for Uighur food—"Uighur" is pronounced like the word "weaker"—which consisted of fatty mutton kabobs over rice. It was a workout for the jaw. Afterward came several bottles of pilsner, locally brewed and superb, which Kyle, demonstrating the advanced level of his Chinese assimilation, deftly opened with a chopstick. Philippe told us about the local skiing options. There are three areas in the region, he said, and tomorrow he recommended a visit to his favorite, a place called Ban Fang Gou—Wooden Shack Gorge. This was Wooden Shack's third winter in operation. Philippe said we would be the first foreigners ever to visit.

◆ ◆ ◆

37

It snowed two inches overnight, and in the morning the city suddenly looked clean and inviting. Up and down the block from our hotel I watched shopkeepers sweep clear the sidewalk with straw whisks. Philippe came by in the minivan and we drove south into the foothills of the Tianshan. Soon there were no other cars, then there were no bicycles, and finally the only tracks on the snowy road were horse prints. We were in a Kazakh region, said Philippe, and at the outer edges of accessible terrain. Any farther in and we'd reach the granite walls of the Tianshan's anchor peaks. The hills here were short and steep and folded into one another, with gorgeous dark spruce forests on the north-facing slopes and skiable meadows on the south. At the base of the hills were mud-brick homes with thatched roofs. Herds of sheep were tended by Kazakh men seated on hairy, bowlegged horses.

The road turned rough and then very rough and then became little more than a riverbed. Soon we were stuck. Three young men emerged from a nearby home to help us. When they saw we were foreigners they insisted we meet the rest of their family and share a pot of tea. Their house was squat and rectangular; the mud bricks had been stuccoed inside and out, and there was glass in the windows, both signs in these parts of a well-off family. Exquisite tapestries sewn with bright flower patterns hung on the walls. The house had electricity, and there was a radio and black-and-white television. Heat came from a wood-burning stove.

There were three rooms. In the main one, a middle-aged woman wearing a shawl and a thick wool skirt was carving up a sheep that had just been slaughtered. Blood glistened on the dusty brick floor; mutton steaks were laid out on a swatch of burlap. Two young boys played a jacks-like game using the sheep's vertebrae.

The patriarch of the family, Mr. Kai, was sitting in a side room on an enormous bed, called a *kang,* made of brick. In China, families often all sleep together in their kang. Mr. Kai said he was 74 years old. He had seven children and many grandchildren, all of whom lived in nearby homes. (China's ethnic minorities are exempt from the nation's strict one-child laws.) I asked him what the secret to a long life was. He jumped up, performed a little jig, and said, in Mandarin, "Exercise!"

Mrs. Kai, who had been carving the sheep, served us tea. One of the sons came in and played a song on a beautiful, ukulele-like instrument called a *donbula.* We talked at length about the relationship between the United States and China. Mr. Kai said it wouldn't be long before the two nations became each other's most important foreign markets. Even out here, there was a resolute sense of China's impending greatness.

Eventually Philippe and the driver went outside and put chains on the minivan, and we continued to the ski hill. At first glance, and even second glance, it is impossible to tell that Wooden Shack Gorge is a ski area. It looked like a

Mongolian herders' encampment. There were four white, round canvas-sided yurts, each with a stovepipe emerging from a conical roof. The yurts bordered a gently sloped meadow that extended for maybe two football-field lengths, lined on both edges with small flags of green and orange cloth. We were at the end of a narrow valley; on three sides of the meadow rose treed hillsides creased with tight drainages. The place appeared abandoned.

Philippe knocked on the metal door of one of the yurts. After a moment the door opened. We had reached the main office.

Mr. Ma was in charge of the ski area. He was grumpy, and understandably so: He had recently hurt his knee and was unable to ski. Inside Mr. Ma's yurt were crammed two beds, a stove, a small selection of cookware, a wooden desk, a television connected to a Chinese-made Micro Genius game system, a red motorcycle helmet, and 100 pairs of skis, boots, and poles. This was the equipment the General Secretary had mentioned. It was indeed Japanese—Yamaha, Nishizawa, Ogasaka—and circa 1980. On busy weekends early in the winter, said Philippe, who had skied here a dozen times this season, every set is often rented out. We paid Mr. Ma the equivalent of $4 each for one night's yurt rental, a dinner that would consist of mutton and rice, and use of the slopes.

Philippe explained that this price did not include the cost of utilizing the lift system. I said there was no lift system. He said there was, indeed. By the time we stepped out of the yurt, word had spread that skiers were at the area, and a half dozen Kazakh herdsmen had gathered, horses in tow. The herdsmen were dressed in wool blazers and wool slacks and beret-style caps. No one wore gloves. Their faces were weather-roughened, with maroon patches on their cheeks that showed evidence of frostbite scars. They had sharper features than the east coast Chinese—aquiline noses, squared jaws. There was much yelling and arm waving. They wanted us to rent their horses. This was the lift system.

Kyle handled the bargaining. Each horse had a separate owner, and each animal's rental had to be negotiated individually. It was a lengthy process that resulted, after much haggling, in a fee of about $1 per person per hour.

Several more herdsmen came running out of nearby homes. They asked to join us on a ski. Of course, we said. I told them my name was Mike. This caused an uproar. "Mike, Mike," they repeated, rocking with laughter. "Mike, Mike, Mike." Evidently, they had never encountered such a peculiar and funny name. Their names, they said, were Silambecha and Muhemiech and Aslavek and Chuman and Nur and Genghis.

Genghis was clearly the leader. He was taller than the others, and even more angular, with a toughened mountain-man presence about him—a piercing gaze, a missing front tooth, a shadowy mustache—that seemed to suggest he would never tire and never complain. He was 30 years old, I learned, and recently married. He seemed knowledgeable about the skiing options and conferred with Kyle. "His suggestion is to ski the waterfall," said Kyle. It was agreed. The herdsmen and Philippe went into the yurt to borrow equipment. Then we all hopped on horses.

With one hand I held my skis over my shoulder, with the other I clutched the reins. My horse was a stout chestnut stallion named Hong La Ma. Our procession, 11 in all, including several horse owners who joined us on foot, ambled single-file up the meadow and into the dark woods. A woman came down the hill with a stick braced across her shoulders and a bucket of water dangling from each end. The path became steeper, and narrow, as we ascended one of the drainages on an ankle-deep layer of snow atop an iced-over river. After a long half hour on horseback, we came to the waterfall. It was more of a frozen cascade, a few hundred feet long, but steep, the ice covered only by a dusting of snow. We dismounted and scrambled to the top of the cascade, grabbing tree limbs to stop ourselves from sliding. The horses started back down with their owners.

At this point I was wondering if the Kazakhs had actually taught themselves to ski. We were probably 500 vertical feet above the meadow, and this was by no means a beginner's run. It wasn't much of a ski run at all—it seemed better suited for ice skates. We all clicked into our gear, and Kyle, Chris, and I stood at the top and watched the herdsmen push off. The Kazakhs *had* taught themselves to ski. Only it was a manner of skiing I had never before encountered. They stood with their skis wide apart and slightly wedged, and arranged their bodies in the sort of heel-heavy squat one uses in an open-pit outhouse. Arms were either thrust straight ahead, sleepwalker style, or else left dangling limply at their sides. And then they each went straight down the fall line, full speed, no turns, over the chattery gray ice until they blew up in frightening heaps. Genghis was the most adept at this. He achieved the deepest squat, the fastest speed, and the most magnificent heap. Philippe, too, utilized the same style. Following each demolition he recited his other English phrase: "Not a problem. Not a problem." No one quite knew what to make of our odd, controlled back-and-forth method of skiing.

I noticed other things. There seemed to be little understanding of proper boot-closure methods; everyone skied with buckles flapping open. Poles were a mysterious accessory, DIN setting a foreign concept, waterproof fabrics completely unknown. Every time Aslavek so much as wiggled his toes he blew out of both skis. He put them back on, blew out again, put them on, and so forth, working his way gradually down the hill. This did not for an instant seem to prevent him from having the time of his life. In fact, everyone looked thrilled.

Though I am a firm adherent of the if-you're-smiling-you're-doing-it-right school of skiing, I was nonetheless concerned that it was only a matter of time before every Wooden Shack regular became permanently crippled. I came up with a plan and discussed it with Kyle and Chris. And when we returned to the yurts, Kyle made an announcement: Anyone interested in a lesson should show up tomorrow at 10 A.M. We would pay everyone's rental and slope-access fee, and demonstrate a different, less body-damaging style of skiing.

♦ ♦ ♦

The morning was blue and warm. While we'd slept cozily in the yurt (Philippe awoke every two hours to feed wood into the stove) it had snowed several more inches. We ate cold mutton for breakfast. From the yurt we overlooked a series of compact pastures bordered by rickety fences, each pasture with a pile of hay bigger than most of the homes.

At 10:15 we still had not seen any sign of other skiers, and I wondered if the Kazakhs had unexpectedly turned timid. But then, as if by design, there began a grand migration. Men galloped up the valley on horses. Others walked in groups of twos and threes. One shepherd, who did not want to miss the lesson but couldn't abandon his flock, simply brought his sheep with him. Another rode in on a donkey. Three of Mr. Kai's grandsons, whom we had met when our van became stuck on the way to the hill, trotted in on stallions. The most theatrical entrance was by a young man named Hadahan, who brought with him his prized ram, which he had festooned with pink ribbons and a gold-embroidered halter and an ornate red-and-black saddle. The ram was hauling a two-wheeled wooden cart containing a felt-covered throne, upon which sat Hadahan's infant son.

A total of 26 skiers showed up, all male. (Feminism has yet to make advances in western China.) The men ranged in age from 16 to 56, the oldest being Genghis's father, Hedarki, who had never before skied. There were about an equal number of spectators, most of them old men with pointy beards smoking long pipes and watching the proceedings with what seemed like scholarly interest.

We made sure everyone wore boots that fit, and were buckled shut, and we adjusted bindings and distributed ski poles. The three of us also donned rental equipment, so the locals wouldn't think we were aided by our flashier-looking gear. And then, with Kyle translating and Chris and I demonstrating, we began the lesson.

The Kazakhs are by nature rugged, intrepid people—natural athletes, really—and they gelled to our version of the sport with remarkable ease. We essentially conducted 26 simultaneous private lessons, dispensing a few pointers, mostly in pantomime, and sending each skier down the meadow. They'd walk back up and we'd hand out more advice. Within two hours, those who had skied before were inscribing nearly clean sets of parentheses on the hill, and actually attempting pole plants once in a while, and occasionally proceeding at slower than the maximum possible velocity. Most of the first-timers locked into snowplows and casually speedboated the meadow. And Genghis, looking Fonz-like in a black leather jacket, became a star, flinging himself off small jumps and hip-angulating with a pizzazz that'd impress Stein Erickson. Several of the stronger skiers promised to pass on advice to others who were unable to show up.

As a finale, we set up a giant-slalom course and staged the first annual Wooden Shack Gorge Invitational Classic, which I timed on my wristwatch. Genghis, racing with a lit cigarette in his mouth and his natty blue cap turned backward, won easily. We had everyone, participants and spectators alike, whooping up a storm and laughing at the mishaps and grinning like game-show contestants, and the place suddenly *felt* like a ski area—happy and silly and spirited—and without needing to translate a single syllable I could tell that the Kazakhs realized that this is precisely how a ski hill is supposed to feel.

After the race, we hummed the ABC Sports Olympic theme song and presented each participant a medal—actually, foil-wrapped chocolate coins we'd purchased in Urumchi. Then, as befits a champion, Genghis sat on the felt-covered throne and the ram pulled him once around the meadow. By the time he came back to the yurt, Genghis had a sly grin on his face. He whispered something to Kyle, who then came over to me and said, "Genghis has an idea."

♦ ♦ ♦

The idea was this: Genghis, who knew the region as well as anyone, wanted to take us on a backcountry trek over the top of a nearby mountain and down into another, more populated valley. It was a trip he'd completed many times in summer but hadn't, until now, felt qualified to do on skis. Our driver could bring the van around and meet us at a hotel there; Philippe, whose skiing had also been transformed, would join us. We could eat at a restaurant that served dishes other than mutton and, in the morning, visit another Wooden Shack–like ski hill. Of course, we accepted.

Genghis dashed back to his home to grab his backpack. This had been assembled from a sturdy plastic bag that, according to its label, once held 25 kilograms of rice. Several of the herdsmen who had attended the lesson donated their horses to the trip, no charge. We'd ride as far as we could, then continue on foot. The horses would return to Wooden Shack with the herdsmen.

I mounted my horse and was handed an elaborate crop, made of braided leather strips tied to an oak handle, inlaid with gold. Others had fashioned crops out of segments of broken ski poles. Someone rolled cigarettes in delicate paper adorned with tiny Chinese characters, and passed them about. It was powerful tobacco, strong as a joint. Then we took off.

This was no waterfall run. There was no one on foot maintaining a leisurely pace, and the horses bolted along the trail at full gallop. My skis bounced painfully on my shoulder and everything in my periphery became a pale green blur and I was exhilarated and terrified in a prickly way you can only achieve when you realize you're no longer in full control, my heart humming on overdrive. It was only when the trail steepened that we finally slowed down, and we rested our horses and ourselves at Genghis's uncle's house, where we sat cross-legged on the kang and drank tea.

Not far up the trail it became too slippery to ride. We shared another round of cigarettes and said good-bye to the herdsmen, and then it was just Chris and Kyle and myself and Genghis and Philippe, deep in the wilderness. Mist threaded through the treetops. The moon was up, a sliver. We talked about Genghis's recent marriage, and about Philippe's French-speaking girlfriend. We told them about ski areas in the United States, and Genghis seemed ready to pack his bags and move to Jackson Hole.

And then we came to the top. The back side was steep, with tight trees and a perplexing double fall line—an expert run by any standards. It plunged at least 2,000 feet through a variety of snow conditions, none of them optimal.

Philippe had some trouble and crashed several times— "not a problem; not a problem"—but I could perceive in his face the growing realization that a sport he had previously considered confined to a few minor pastures was now boundless. He looked as though he had just won the lottery.

Genghis was something else. He blazed the route, which was undoubtedly a first descent, and I stayed behind him the whole way, mirroring his turns. With each new situation— crusty snow, a brief uphill, a sudden drop-off—I could actually see him improve, his mind piecing together the scattered bits of guidance he had picked up. He'd attempt one or two uncomfortable moves and then swiftly adjust. There was something in the way he skied, a raw fearlessness, an innate sense of flow—a certain rhythm to his skiing that can't be taught—that made me think the General Secretary might be right. Before long, I realized, one of these people is going to be downhill champion of the world.

Have Gun, Will Telemark

"Low reg," said Captain Buzby to the barber. The barber nodded, and the electric razor was at my head like a pit bull. The whole procedure, a standard military low-regulation cut, took three minutes. It reduced my hair from a shoulder-length mop to a dome of uneven stubble. "Now you're in the Marines," said Captain Buzby.

Thus began my stay at the Marine Corps Mountain Warfare Training Center. The center, established in 1951 during the Korean War, is spread over 46,000 remote acres in California's High Sierra, a little north of Mammoth Mountain. Each year, several thousand Marines are put through the four-week Winter Mountain Operations course, most of it conducted in the backcountry on telemark gear, in order to learn how to survive, maneuver, and fight in alpine terrain. It is not inconceivable that the United States, in its role as global cop, will find itself in a skirmish in a mountainous area. I was curious to see how our armed forces prepared themselves for such an encounter.

Captain Buzby, who is stationed full-time at the training center, was responsible for cutting through the red tape and arranging to have me participate in the Winter Mountain Operations course. I'd be joining 750 soldiers from the 2nd Marine Regiment who were training for a tour of duty in Norway. I had never served in the military, and I mentioned that I wanted as authentic an experience as possible. Buzby said—a little too eagerly, I felt—that he was more than willing to accommodate me.

The majority of the Mountain Warfare Center is located above 10,000 feet, in a region of granite-peaked mountains, high-alpine valleys, and wind-bent stands of fir and juniper and ponderosa pine. The center's entrance sign displays a skier carrying a machine gun. When I arrived at the base, snow was piled on the sides of the roads in drifts that could bury a flagpole. I passed a small city of green canvas tents; a collection of camouflage-painted snow cats; and a dual-rotored helicopter big enough to hold a high school gymnasium. I met Captain Buzby in the center's headquarters, a tan cinderblock building. He took one look at my hair and marched me to the barber.

Second stop was the supply warehouse. Captain Buzby barked commands at the soldier behind the counter and equipment was flung at me left and right: long johns, jacket, pants, gloves, sleeping bag, canteen, stove, cook set, spoon, compass, first-aid kit, day pack, expedition pack, and so on. Everything was brown or green or camo-colored.

Then we went to the equipment room to find ski gear. I was given a pair of white uninsulated VB (vapor-barrier) boots, which were essentially rubber L.L. Bean duck boots with squared-off toes that could accommodate telemark bindings. My poles were of the 1960s variety, with leather straps and baskets the diameter of Frisbees. My skis were pure white, 200 centimeters long, manufactured by a company called Karhu. Both skis were labeled "left," but I didn't mention this to Buzby. I feared he'd have me doing push-ups all night for insubordination.

I carried all my stuff—it weighed nearly 100 pounds—to the Bachelor Officers' Quarters, where I was given a dorm for the night. "Be out front at zero-five-hundred," said Buzby. I'd be catching a snow-cat ride to meet my company, which had already been in the field for several days. Captain Buzby wouldn't be joining me; he had a few days' leave. "Bad weather's coming," he said. Then he left.

It was still dark when I put on my forest-colored camouflaged ski outfit (known on base as a tree suit), stuffed my pack, and caught the cat. Marines call snow cats "BV-206s," though nobody could tell me exactly why. I sat in the enclosed back compartment with four soldiers. The ride took about an hour. Three of the men spent the whole time attempting to convince the fourth that the South actually won the Civil War. The conversation was densely expletive-laden; it made any locker-room banter I'd ever witnessed seem downright courteous. I didn't say much.

I was dropped off at a broad, treeless meadow called Silver Creek, 11,500 feet above sea level. This was temporary home to the 90 soldiers of Alpha Company—my company. The sky was cloudless; the temperature was just below freezing. Helicopters swirled overhead. Soldiers in tree suits carrying machine guns and grenade launchers scurried about, saluting one other. There was a field of white dome tents, hardly noticeable in the snow, and a cluster of green, canvas-walled officers' tents. Everywhere, military-issue skis were stuck into the snow, scattered like old fence posts. I was a little spooked. It felt as if Aspen had imposed martial law.

Two of Alpha Company's commanding officers, Sergeants Ramirez and Martinez, introduced themselves. I tried my first-ever salute, but it came off poorly, as if I were attempting to raise my hand in class while scratching my forehead. Ramirez and Martinez gave me a brief tour. I was shown the pee tree and the shit bag. "We don't leave solid waste on the ground," Martinez said. "Too easy for the enemy to track us." He explained that we were participating in a war game with one of the other companies. "Worst job in the military is the guy who has to haul the bag when we move camp."

Ramirez and Martinez also informed me about the Hats and the Neds. Hats are the instructors. They all wear red wool ski caps that stand out like beacons. They're in charge. Whatever they say, you do without question. Everyone else is a Ned, which stands for noneducated dude. Ramirez and Martinez were Hats. I was a complete Ned.

I caught up with the rest of the Alpha Company Neds as they were learning to be towed on skis behind a BV-206. This is an important skill, a Hat explained, because it enables an entire company to move swiftly with little energy expenditure. One problem: The energy expended by my fellow company-mates was anything but low. For many soldiers, the Winter Mountain Operations course is the first time they have ever seen snow, let alone skied it. I witnessed face plants, butt bounces, somersaults, and multi-Marine pileups. One soldier split his lip on the tip of his ski, opening a gash that required six stitches. Another blackened his eye when he fell against the handle of his ski pole. Everyone moaned about the cold. The 10th Mountain Division these guys ain't. If Russia all of a sudden decided to attack the Rockies, we'd be paying for Telluride tickets in rubles.

Next came a lesson on snow-cave building. I learned the secrets of a top-notch cave—one with a cooking level, a sleeping shelf, ventilation holes, and a draftproof door. I also discovered how to hoo-ya like a pro. In the Marines, "hoo-ya" means "What's up?"; "Do you understand me?"; "Are you okay?"; and about a million other things. When a superior officer asks, "Hoo-ya?," which happens every 30 seconds, the only appropriate response is, "Hoo-ya, sir!" If you learn anything in the Marines, you learn how to hoo-ya.

After the snow-cave class, we were broken up into groups of four and told to dig our own caves. I was teamed with three lieutenant corporals—Hamel, Pelkey, and Krohn. We dug feverishly. A cave that can hold four people, two M16s, one M60, three stoves, four sets of ski gear, and four bloated backpacks is no simple excavation. By the time we were done, the place was a subterranean living room. We even sculpted a TV at the far end (yes, we made cracks about the snowy reception). Hats came around and made sure our creation was sturdy enough and so well hidden that the enemy could march right over it and not know we were there. "Good job," one Hat said. "Now you're going to spend the night in there."

Marine snow-cave rules dictate that one person must remain awake at all times, to make sure ventilation holes don't clog and to detect the presence of the enemy. But it was too cold for any of us to sleep—the temperature dropped below zero as night fell—so we stayed up all night talking, while gradually getting drenched from water dripping off the cave's ceiling.

"This is the hardest thing I've ever done in the Marines," said Hamel. "It's ten times worse than boot camp. Maybe twenty. I hope I break a bone so I can get out of here."

Suggested Krohn: "You could always drink your stove fuel."

We talked about our lousy haircuts, our nonexistent love lives, our foolish jobs. I learned that there was such an extreme tobacco shortage at camp that six cigarettes were selling for $10. Pelkey knew one guy who'd been chewing the same wad of Copenhagen for three days. "He stores it in its tin overnight," Pelkey told us. We listened to determine whose teeth chattered the loudest. We placed bets on how many toes we'd each lose to frostbite. I guessed seven. We pretended to watch our TV, taking turns filling in the dialogue. I learned how to assemble and disassemble an M60 machine gun. And of course, we all swore a lot.

When we were too chilled to speak, we fired up the stoves and ate. There is much lore concerning armed-forces gruel. It's been called pig slop, sewer soup, mystery meat—any gustatory insult you can name. I can now confirm that it is truly deserved. Our meals, called RCWs (Rations, Cold Weather) came in white plastic bags, with the contents labeled, often in an odd syntax, on the front in block letters. Ration 4B, for example, read:

CHICKEN A LA KING

COOKIE CHOCOLATE COVERED

GRANOLA BAR AND OATMEAL COOKIE BAR

CHOCOLATE DISK

BEVERAGE BASE: ORANGE.

I know: Doesn't sound so bad. But open the package. The chicken, shredded and freeze dried, looks like moldy Rice Krispies. The cookie is bulletproof—each bite requires several minutes of chewing. The granola and oatmeal bars could moonlight as mah-jongg tiles. Chocolate disk: hockey puck. And the beverage base, I'm convinced, is actually *Agent* Orange.

The next morning, at 0530, I went helicopter skiing. Sort of. I left my cave-mates and joined Captain Scott Fuller's 29-man platoon. It was snowing as hard as snow can fall—two inches an hour, at least. As we awaited our ride, I was told in graphic detail how a helicopter carrying several Marines had crashed at this very spot last year. Everyone on board was killed. One soldier even pointed out the sheared-off trees. "The harder it's snowing," he said, "the greater the likelihood of a crash." That's when the helicopter arrived. It was the portly one I'd seen at the headquarters, the one that looked about as aerodynamic as a K-Mart.

It was too late to back out. The whirlybird landed, the back popped open, and the commanding officers herded us aboard, yelling over the rotors' din. "Skis—there! Packs—there! Butts—there! Belts—on! Helmets—on! Go!" The helicopter strained to lift off, wrestling with gravity, swaying violently in the blustering winds. The copter seemed bungeed to the earth. But the machine managed to outmuscle Mother Nature, and a minute later we landed atop a treeless ridge.

The exercise was backcountry troop movement. I was assigned to the brakeman position on a large sled, which could be used to transport wounded soldiers. The sled's frontman was Gunnery Sergeant Howe. Working together, Howe and I managed to perform something of an Abbot and Costello routine. By the time we got back to camp, we had dented the sled, lacerated our knees, ripped our pants, broken an M16, and destroyed a half dozen fir saplings. Captain Fuller was less than pleased.

Back at Silver Creek, where a 200-vertical-foot poma serviced a gentle slope, it was time for mandatory ski instruction. We attempted to solve our equipment mysteries. VB boots—which the men called bubble boots—are so soft you can almost touch your ankle to the snow without rolling your ski onto edge. Basically, wearing bubble boots is akin to skiing barefoot, except your feet don't get as cold. Not an easy thing to master, especially on telemark gear.

It took me a dozen runs to figure out a workable turn—gradually sliding my downhill ski forward while lowering my inside knee, accompanied by a quick plant of both poles. Not pretty, but effective. I marveled as one officer, Sergeant Beard, blew by me, performing dazzling, aggressive tele turns, dropped knee dragging elegantly in the powder. He was wearing bubble boots and a loaded pack, and hauling behind him a full-length rescue sled.

Alas, things soon got serious. An attack, the commanding officers felt, was imminent, so we shifted immediately into tactical mode. We covered ourselves with overwhites, stationed guards throughout camp, and moved about silently. Sleep was out of the question. From 10 P.M. to midnight, I was assigned fire watch. From midnight to two, I was on camp patrol. From two to three, I was given guard duty. Still, the enemy didn't show.

Then, at three—as I was approaching 48 sleepless hours— I was drafted to join a seven-man squad on a reconnaissance mission deep into the woods, in search of enemy outposts. We were not allowed to use flashlights, even though snow was still pounding down. So we stumbled in the dark for hours, in the process shorting out our field radio and nearly breaking our skis tumbling into tree wells. We found no sign of the enemy.

When we returned home, the commanding officer was furious. Our failure to maintain communication had set off a frenzy in camp. Delirious with exhaustion, we stood slack-jawed as the officer berated us. "There will be no sleep for you," we were informed, and as punishment all of us were immediately placed on extra guard duty. We marched around camp until dawn.

Finally, after downing Ration 5A for breakfast—OATMEAL (STRAWBERRY)—my abbreviated tour of duty came to an end. I excused myself from my squad, packed my gear, said goodbye to my commanding officers and cave-mates, and set off on the long slog back to headquarters, following the cat road. The sun soon burned through the clouds, and I started to defrost. And when I eventually came upon the cinderblock buildings of the Warfare Training Center and saw my vehicle, I felt an overwhelming surge of relief. The Marines may have stolen my hair, but I had regained my freedom.

The Ahab of Kilimanjaro

Nobody understood. The entire village of Umbwe, Tanzania, maybe 20 people, surrounded me, staring at the strange, crazily colored objects lying on the grass. Brows furrowed; eyes squinted. Not a hint of comprehension. I was gesticulating wildly—I didn't speak a word of Wachagga, Umbwe's native tongue, and my ten phrases of Swahili got me nowhere. None of them, I'm sure, had seen ski equipment before. None even knew the sport of skiing existed. But they desperately wanted to understand: What on earth was a *wazungu*—a white person—doing here, at the base of Mount Kilimanjaro, with this pile of odd-looking gear?

I pulled one man, who seemed less shy than the rest, toward me. He was small, with skin the color of a walnut and legs as thin as baseball bats. I kneeled down and removed one of his sandals, made of a piece of rubber cut from an old car tire. I put his foot into one of my bright orange ski boots and buckled it up. The crowd laughed nervously. I put the other one on him. More laughter, louder. Families from neighboring villages were running up the dirt road to see what was going on. Forty people were there. It was nearly sunset in the jungle. Pink light fringed the broad fronds of the banana trees; bugs screeched like a freighter pulling into a siding. Kilimanjaro stood huge and looming above us, head in the clouds, only a brief piece of the lower glaciers visible. I snapped the man into my bindings and slid his hands through my pole straps. Hilarity. I pushed him slowly down the grass slope. Pandemonium. Fifty people were watching, maybe more. I pointed to the top of Kili, to the snow. I pushed the man some more. I pointed again.

A young boy in the front wearing a shirt fashioned from a burlap bag was the first to understand. He assumed a look on his face as if he'd just swallowed a peach pit. He whispered to the girl standing next to him. Her mouth dropped. The crowd buzzed with hushed conversation, then fell silent. They understood. *The wazungu is going to take the things up the mountain and then ride down the snow.* It seemed to them an absolutely illogical thing to do, yet they understood. Smiles of recognition blossomed. Every culture has its silly games, and this, they figured, was one my culture embraced. They seemed to approve. For more than an hour, in groups of twos and threes, they came up and touched the equipment, then looked skyward in the direction of Kili, nodding their heads. They did this until dark, still glancing upward even when they couldn't see the mountain anymore.

The inspiration came from Ernest Hemingway, an apt person to be the progenitor of large-scale foolishness. A few summers ago, while browsing my local used-book store, I came upon a well-known collection of Hemingway's short stories. Its title: *The Snows of Kilimanjaro.* Seeing the word "Snows" made my blood jump. Seeing it near the word "Kilimanjaro"—a mountain, I knew, that was the tallest in Africa—created a double jump. In an instant, a notion took root in my head.

The first problem was finding out if skiing Kilimanjaro was actually feasible. I called people at the Tanzanian embassy; I spoke with expert mountaineers; I consulted professional guides. No one could tell me if sliding down Kili was possible: None had climbed it with an eye toward skiing. Several people, however, politely informed me that it was impossible. The slopes were too steep, the effort required was too large, the snowfall was too unpredictable. But the more I was told it couldn't be done, the more I wanted to go. Skiing in Africa seemed so wonderfully *wrong,* it thrilled every renegade ski cell in my body. It was an obsession. I became the Ahab of Kilimanjaro.

For a year, though, I got nowhere. Potential travel partners thought I was loopy. Outfitters laughed at me over the phone. My father mailed me life insurance forms. Then, in a two-week frenzy, everything clicked. First I discovered a London-based guide service, Executive Wilderness Programmes, that was willing to arrange the trip. "To the best of my knowledge, a ski descent of Kili has never been attempted before," wrote the company's owner, Ian Munro, in a codicil to our agreement. "There might be a very good reason for this . . ." he added, concluding the thought with an ominous ellipsis. I immediately signed the contract. Then I conscripted a close friend, intrepid photographer Hank de Vré, to join me. We were shot silly with vaccines—yellow fever, diphtheria, rabies, tetanus, typhoid, hepatitis, meningitis—then grappled with the cryptic application for a Tanzanian visa. (Question 14: *What proof have you provided to support the stated purpose of your intended visit?*) We compiled camping gear, climbing gear, skiing gear, camera gear, hot-weather gear, cold-weather gear, and in-between-weather gear. We packed a grand total of 11 pieces of luggage. Then, in late June, the best time for cooperative weather on Kilimanjaro, we departed for Africa.

◆ ◆ ◆

We flew over the Atlantic, Europe, and the Sahara before bouncing down at Jomo Kenyatta International Airport in Nairobi, Kenya. Kilimanjaro is 150 miles south of Nairobi, just below the Tanzanian border. We shuffled through a gauntlet of visa stampers and passport checkers and machine-gun-toting inspectors, then arrived in the baggage claim area. Ten of our bags completed the journey. The eleventh, containing all of Hank's climbing gear, was somewhere in the ether. Just as the first twinges of panic struck, we met Chris Muriithi, our Kilimanjaro guide, who had come to pick us up.

Chris led us to a wooden counter tucked into a corner of the airport, and Hank and I filled out a Property Irregularity Report. The person manning the counter stuck the report, restaurant-tab style, onto a long nail. No chance of ever seeing that bag again, I thought.

We drove, with 91 percent of our luggage, through downtown Nairobi in Chris's well-worn Toyota Land Cruiser. It was nearly midnight, but the outside air felt thick and clingy. Chris cheered us up. He had the type of face that was preternaturally disposed to smiling: rounded with permanent baby fat and embellished with a tiny mustache that seemed a parody of full-blown mustaches and clownish eyebrows that leapt upward in charcoal-colored circumflexes. He was 34 years old, he told us, in British-inflected English, the son of a Zulu father and Kikuyu mother. He grew up in Kenya but spent much of his teens perfecting his climbing techniques in the German Alps. He'd been a professional guide for a dozen years, and this was his most intriguing assignment, he said, since guiding Jimmy Carter halfway up Kilimanjaro a decade ago.

We slept four hours at the Panafric Hotel while Chris searched Nairobi for replacement climbing gear. It is no easy task finding mountaineering equipment in the middle of the night in the middle of Africa, and the stuff Chris did gather looked like surplus from the War of 1812. Good enough, we figured, and lashed all our bags to the roof of the crowded early-morning bus into Tanzania.

East Africans seem, for the most part, to have a relaxed attitude toward life, summed up by the Swahili expression *pole, pole*—"slowly, slowly." There is, though, one glaring exception to their mellowness. They drive as if they can't wait another instant to meet their maker. The bus on which Hank and Chris and I rode hurtled down a one-and-a-half-lane wide, pothole-infested highway at speeds normally employed by electricity. Our driver, so far as I could tell, followed only two rules: Hit the horn, not the brake; and play chicken with any approaching vehicle until it pulls onto the embankment.

The roadsides were packed with people, some riding donkeys, some on ancient black Schwinns, some balancing bushels of bananas or buckets of water on their heads. We were traveling through Masai territory, and scattered across the scrubby rangelands were herds of cattle, kicking up thin clouds of amber dust, tended by young boys wearing free-flowing, blood-red robes. "One herd for each wife," Chris said, explaining that polygamy is common in East Africa. Even the president of Tanzania, Ali Hassan Mwinyi, has three wives. We passed a few villages, clusters of mushroom-shaped homes with walls made of cow dung and roofs of banana leaves. The Masai women stared at us as we rumbled by; I stared back, gaping at their extraordinary earlobes, which were stretched into teardrop-shaped loops large enough to admit a cucumber.

All along the road were zebra—more common here than deer are in New England—as well as flocks of ostrich: great brown meatballs balanced on pairs of toothpicks. Our bus once swerved (surprisingly) to avoid a group of giraffes, who galloped into the brush with funny, loping strides, their magnificent necks chugging up and down like oil rigs. We passed coffee bushes, sugar-cane fields, and cypress groves. Dimensions I'd come to accept as standard were no longer valid. Everything seemed bigger. Thorns on acacia trees were the size of railroad spikes; sunflowers were as tall as telephone poles; birds were larger than people. We saw several massive baobab trees, with twisted trunks thicker than grain silos. Most startling of all, though, were the termite hills. These mounds of freshly churned earth were often 15 feet tall—I had to ask Chris what they were—and they dotted the landscape like haystacks in the Midwest. If you'd need crampons and an ice ax to climb the East African termite hills, I thought, what could the mountains possibly be like?

Moments later, I had my answer. A few miles before the Tanzanian border, Chris squeezed my hand and pointed to the southern horizon. I squinted hard, saw nothing, and he nudged my chin up slightly and it took shape before me, sharpening gradually against the pale blue sky like a Polaroid photo. My head was tipped at an angle usually reserved for shooting stars, and there, in front of me, rising like a separate continent from the East African jungle, rising through two strata of cloud layers, rising until the top was splashed with snow, was Kilimanjaro.

◆ ◆ ◆

Many Tanzanians believe nobody has ever climbed Kili. Thousands of people have, of course (it was first summited in 1887), and there are photographs to prove it. Still, the belief persists. And when you are in the city of Moshi, the supply center for Kilimanjaro climbs, this belief is entirely feasible. Moshi is three degrees south of the equator and, as the crow flies, 16 miles from Kilimanjaro's summit. In this small distance the climate shifts, against all probability, from permanent heat to permanent snow. Moshi is 2,900 feet above sea level; the top of Kili is 19,340. This base-to-summit rise of more than three vertical miles is one of the greatest in the world—far greater than Everest's. Standing in Moshi's town square and staring at Kilimanjaro's glaciers prompts such strong feelings of disbelief that you fear you're suffering from the onset of malaria. And since Kili rises alone—it's an active volcano not part of any mountain range—it appears even more unearthly, a kind of giant geological mutation.

Moshi is where our troubles began. Just as we were making final plans for our ascent—hiring porters, organizing

equipment, purchasing food—Chris discovered, while regis-
tering our climb with the park service, that a new rule governing activity on Kilimanjaro had recently been established.
It was a simple rule. The Tanzanian government, in an effort
to reduce the death rate on Kili, had banned all sports
equipment not directly related to climbing. This included
hang gliders, mountain bikes, and—go figure—ski gear.
Skiing not permitted on Kilimanjaro? In my months of
preparation, the idea had never crossed my mind. A wave of
vertigo overtook me, and I suddenly felt ill.

I tried to get the director general of the Tanzanian national parks on the phone, to beg for a special dispensation. His
secretary answered the call, and just as the director was
about to get on the line, the phone went dead. I tried a half
dozen times to call back; no luck. The phone could be out
for days, Chris told me. We had no choice. We'd have to visit
the director in person, back near the Kenyan border, in the
city of Arusha.

The next morning we awoke at five and walked to the
Moshi bus station. Even at this hour the place was a mad-
house, teeming with vendors selling everything imaginable
and several things not: snakebite tablets, hard-boiled eggs,
sad-eyed burros, sides of beef, broken watches, three-month-
old Taiwanese newspapers, human teeth. The ramshackle
buses, each independently owned, were painted in brilliant
swirls of color; hawkers shouted destinations and drivers
leaned on horns. Every few minutes another bus would

lurch drunkenly into the station, spewing clouds of black exhaust, and the crowd would scramble to make way. Chris guided us to a van-size vehicle that had tires 50,000 miles beyond bald, and we got on. A swarm of trinket sellers, who had followed us, engulfed our bus; hands clutching silver bracelets and beaded necklaces and leather doodads were thrust through our window. There were 18 seats on the bus, and when 36 people had boarded we finally took off, at typical breakneck speed, road dust pouring in through the open windows.

Three hours later we arrived, soaked in sweat, in front of a great concrete edifice called the Arusha International Conference Center. We walked up to the sixth floor, to room 618. The director general himself answered the door, and we stood in his reception room and told him our problem. He responded, in English, with the following words: "No skiing, no skiing, no skiing." He was a large man, fat, with linebacker's shoulders and a firm, laconic manner. His voice was calm and confident, and as he spoke his head moved slowly back and forth, as if to say, Don't even try to persuade me otherwise.

Chris requested a private meeting in his office, and Mr. Melamari—he never told us his first name—settled in behind his huge mahogany desk. I handed him a baseball cap as a gift; he pushed it aside, unimpressed, next to a small ebony carving of an elephant. He nodded at me, and I began to beg. I explained how far we'd come, how important this journey was, how I'd been unaware of the new rules. Mr. Melamari didn't say anything. When I finished my spiel he sat back in his chair, and the room was silent for a good 60 seconds. The taste of bile burned my throat. Finally, he opened a drawer, took out a black pen, and began writing on our climbing permit. He wrote for a few moments, then handed the paper back to me. I sucked in my breath. "Permission has been granted for them to use the equipment," it said. I exhaled, and we shook hands.

Back in Moshi, we learned more good news: Hank's missing bag had been discovered. It had been in Amsterdam doing God knows what and, for a small fortune, had been driven to our hotel. We quickly packed our stuff, hired a group of porters, and crammed everyone into a pair of old Land Rovers. Then we rumbled into the jungle, aiming for the head of the Umbwe route, a steep and rarely climbed path up Kili's southwestern face. (Nearly all Kili climbers use the so-called tourist route, a long and gentle climb up the eastern flank. I wanted to avoid the crowds.) The road was essentially an extra-wide hiking path, covered with boulders and fallen branches, cut through jungle thick with mango trees and bamboo stands and ferns with fronds as big as beach towels.

It took almost four hours to drive the 40 miles to Umbwe. Everyone in town came out to see who had arrived, and after I went through my elaborate skiing demonstration, a small celebration ensued. A jar of "banana juice"—highly alcoholic moonshine made from overripe bananas and sorghum—was passed around, along with a pipe full of a Tanzanian bright-green ganja. The children of Umbwe, once they trusted me, were gregarious, fascinated with my hiking boots and eyeglasses and camera and wazungu hair. One girl showed me the scythe she used to cut bamboo. I showed her my Swiss army knife. Hank handed out squares of Hershey bars—the kids' first taste of chocolate—and they brought us coffee beans fresh off the tree, showing us how to peel the beans and eat them raw.

That night, I collapsed in my tent, exhausted. I was pimple-faced and bug bitten and sour-stomached, and I still had no clue if skiing Kili was even possible. But at least I had permission to find out. It was time to begin the climb.

◆ ◆ ◆

The morning dawned misty, the treetops shrouded in fog. Once in a while the leaves would shake violently as a black-and-white colobus monkey leapt from branch to branch. It was steam-room hot. We were all fully loaded, Hank and Chris and I wearing packs on our back, the porters opting for the head-balancing technique. We had hired 10 porters to join us on the journey—with all our food and extra gear (and some good-natured featherbedding), that's how many were necessary—and we formed a long, single-file line, stopping often to roll downed trees out of the way. The path was treacherous: expert-slope steep and slick with mud. Traction was nil. Within a mile, I had tumbled a half dozen times.

Never, during the entire trip, did I see a porter fall. I didn't even see one stumble. Their balance was eerily amazing. And they were wearing shoes that Americans would've thrown away. In fact, many were received used from relief agencies: treadless sneakers, worn-out docksiders, rubber boots held together with masking tape, old flip-flops. One man, Edward, was hiking in a brown blazer—complete with pen in the breast pocket—as well as slacks, a yellow button-down, and black loafers. Our biggest porter, Method, built like a redwood, wore my ski bag on his head as if it were nothing more than an oddly designed baseball cap. When I asked him how it felt, he joked—in pantomime—that the weight on his head was making him a little shorter with every step.

I hiked at my own pace. The jungle seemed to breathe. It was so tightly packed with life—trees, flowers, birds, vines, bugs—that my presence almost felt intrusive. The ground, where it wasn't muddy, was soft as a trampoline. Light filtered through the canopy in scattered spangles. The air smelled so fertile I felt as though I could toss some spores into the sky and full-grown ferns would float down. I tramped around giant beds of wild roses, watched insects become tangled in spiderwebs vast as fishing nets, and saw two wild boars hightail it into the mist.

We camped our first night at 9,350 feet, near a stream of glacial runoff. By the time Hank and I arrived, camp was already set up; dinner—beef and potatoes—had been cooked; and the porters were involved in a heated game of poker, folding their hands with dramatic exasperation onto a flat rock. One of the porters, Godfrey, had an old transistor radio tuned to a station playing Zairian soukous music— a kind of infectiously upbeat techno-reggae. Just before bed, the porters filled a large pot with water, put all their socks into it, and waited for the water to boil. When it did, they removed their socks, chanted a brief song, and each drank a cup of sock soup. Our language barrier prevented me from discerning what exactly was the significance of this ritual, and so the meaning of the sock water remains a mystery, but I suspect it may be the secret to their phenomenal fitness.

A jumble of high-pitched birdcalls awoke me. We broke camp swiftly, happy in the flush morning light, and rejoined the path. It was still T-shirt weather. The way soon grew steep, and I needed to use rocks and roots as handholds. The jungle ended, substituted with a forest of short, thin heather trees and piles of volcanic rock.

Camp two was established at 13,000 feet, in a forest of giant groundsels. The giant groundsel, found only on Kilimanjaro and Mount Kenya, looks like something Dr. Seuss might've concocted. It is about 20 feet tall; it emerges from the earth as a tree, becomes a cactus after a few feet, and, just before its top, swells into mass of dried vegetation resembling the loaf of meat that sits on a spit in a gyro shop. This is crowned with an artichoke-like cluster of leaves. Once every 50 to 70 years, Chris told me, the groundsel blooms with flowers that resemble ears of corn.

Dinner was rice and carrots and a curious corn-based concoction called *ugali*. Ugali is pronounced "ooh, golly," as in "ooh, golly, is this bland." It is oatmeal-colored and has the same malleability as Play-Doh. The porters seemed to love it; most of mine was surreptitiously fed to the white-necked ravens that accompanied us in camp. Communication with the porters was difficult. None spoke much English, though they all referred to themselves using anglicized versions of their Wachagga names. But after dinner I introduced them all to the international language of Frisbee. Within five minutes they had the hang of it, and my yellow Frisbee soared around camp, everybody doubled with laughter each time someone tried to catch it behind his back or under his legs or when it lodged in a groundsel. We played until it was too dark to see.

A layer of frost was on the ground when we awoke. We climbed out of the groundsel forest, and the vegetation petered out. A few hundred feet above camp the only signs of life were tiny star-shaped cacti and clusters of yellow sunflecks, flowers small enough to be potted in a thimble. Mostly it was volcanic rock. Soon there was no flora at all, just Mars-red soil and black pebbles that crunched beneath our boots in a military cadence. At 15,000 feet, we reached the first bit of snow. I promptly created my first African snowball, big as a melon, and threw it at Hank.

This was the highest I had ever ventured, and the altitude began to affect me. My body throbbed as though I were standing in front of a powerful speaker, bombarded by silent bass lines. My steps became slow, deliberate. Mini headaches strobed through my brain, like pinpricks. We set up camp at 16,000 feet on a sandy spot beneath the Little Breach glacier. It was snowing and foggy; Kili's summit was hidden. This was as high as the porters could venture: They had no warm clothing. We took a bit of food, all our cold-weather gear, and one set of ski equipment. Hank, who had originally planned to ski, decided he couldn't carry both skis and cameras. Our stove was irreparably clogged, so in order to melt ice for water, we also took whatever firewood was hauled up. Then the porters descended, leaving Chris, Hank, and me alone on Kilimanjaro.

We pitched the tent, started a fire, made tea. We were smelly and weary and unshaven. To prevent ailments that could jeopardize the climb, we began popping pills like addicts: Diamox, Tylenol, Phenergan, Sudafed, Keflex, Imodium (altitude sickness, headache, nausea, runny nose, sore throat, diarrhea). We studied the topos and made plans for an early-morning summit attempt: We'd leave at midnight when the scree would be frozen and easier to negotiate. The sun dipped behind a ridge and the temperature plunged. We zipped ourselves into our sleeping bags. My heart pounded so heavily I could hear it echoing in my bag. I slipped in and out of consciousness, more than once sitting up, gasping for air.

When the alarm on my watch beeped, I was the first one out of the tent. It was bitter cold. The Southern Cross blazed at maximum wattage, headlining for a full-bore Milky Way. A pair of shooting stars streaked across the heavens—in Swahili, they're called *kibonna omu:* "seen by one." The final 3,000 feet of Kili were visible in the starlight. The summit ridgeline, spiked with arêtes, was silhouetted against the sky. And the famous glaciers—the Heim, the Kersten, the Breach, the Balletto—spilled toward me, shining like reflectors. All of them ended in dramatic black cliffs; none looked even remotely skiable. I stared, shivering and despondent. Maybe, I hoped, maybe the back side of the mountain was skiable. Maybe not. There was nothing I could do but climb.

Hank and Chris arose, and we lit a fire. Using our axes, we hacked out a chunk of ice, melted it in the pot, and made tea. Bits of the previous night's potato stew floated in it, and it made me nauseous. Still, we melted as much ice as possible, and when the wood was gone we had only about a quart of water each in our canteens—a dangerously small quantity for what promised to be an arduous climb.

Headlamps on, the three of us started up the steep, rocky slope, picking our way between the glaciers. My pack, weighed down by a pair of skis and boots, felt obscenely heavy. The tails of my skis dug into my calves with every big step up; the tips, when I was scrambling, scraped against rocks. These frustrations sapped my energy. After an hour of steady climbing, I could feel my body shutting down. My lungs burned. A film of ice covered everything, and I had to be sure of each footfall: We were hiking above cliffs, sometimes chipping out steps with our ice axes, and a slip could be deadly. No one spoke.

We climbed all night, 2,700 vertical feet of unending steepness, and then emerged on the broad plateau-like caldera beneath Kili's summit tower just as the sun crested the far side of the mountain. The world spread before us. Miles below were endless fields of green—the East African veldt. The view was so encompassing we could clearly see the curve of the Earth. An enormous shadow, in the shape of an inverted V, stretched to the horizon—the shadow of Kilimanjaro. Here, three and a half miles above sea level, virtually all the suspended dust particles that give the sky its baby-blue color were beneath us. The sky over Kili was space-blue.

We trudged across the brown caldera, where the warmth of Kili's volcanic belly prevents glaciation, and marveled at the walls of rippled ice, some 300 feet high, that marked the tops of the great glaciers. As the sun rose the ice made angry popping noises, loud as firecrackers.

The last 500 feet were a long, gradual slog to the rounded summit. We saw a few other climbers—the first we'd seen the whole trip—making their way toward us from the tourist route. My drinking water was finished and my saliva had turned the consistency of Elmer's glue. I ached to put a handful of snow in my mouth but I knew that the energy required to melt it would make my body even more dehydrated. As it was, my peripheral vision was gone, vanished in thin air. Thoughts floated through my brain in slow motion, like giant barges, then sunk into my gray matter half-completed. I walked like a drunk.

I was resting against a rock, two thirds of the way up, when my knees buckled and in an instant I was lying on top of my pack, legs flailing, like an overturned turtle. I unclipped my waist and sternum straps, rolled off the pack, and fell asleep. Chris and Hank, who had been hiking a few minutes behind, woke me up. I tried to put my pack back on, but I couldn't even lift it. I was swooning with dizziness. There was no way I could haul my skis to the summit. Chris would have none of it. He lifted my pack, shouldered it, and marched on. Hank and I stumbled along behind. A few minutes later we crept over a dome-shaped mound of boulders and saw a wooden sign that said Uhuru Point—Peace Point. There was no more up. We had summited Kilimanjaro.

"*Thaai,*" whispered Chris, speaking a Kikuyu word that encapsulates a thousand transcendent feelings in one perfect syllable, and is a slightly more reverential version of the English phrase "holy shit." The three of us embraced. Cool air blowing over the summit slapped me from my stupor, and I spun slowly around. That's when I noticed. An exalted thought danced in my mind, tugging my chapped lips into a smile: *skiing.* I spun again, to make sure. Yes. Kili, it turns out, is extraordinarily skiable. Easy descents on the summit icefields, narrow couloirs into the central crater, triple diamonds down the southern glaciers. It didn't seem possible on the way up, but Kilimanjaro has plenty of skiing.

I removed my gear from my pack and put on my ski boots. The snow began a few feet shy of the top, so I dragged my skis over and set them up. I stepped into each binding, the clicks seeming to reverberate long and loud. I stretched for a moment, giddy with anticipation, then gripped my poles and pushed off.

Skiing at 19,000 feet, I promptly discovered, is exhausting. Blinking your eyes at 19,000 feet is exhausting. Your mind is fogged. What is second nature at normal elevation—pole plants, weight shifts, hip angulation—now seems like an impossible puzzle. At extreme altitude, the absurdity of skiing—long things on your feet, long things in your hands—is crystallized. You see why your nonskiing friends make fun of you. I fought my way through two or three turns, yanking my tails around unnaturally, twisting my shoulders like a wrestler trying to break a hold. Ugly skiing; survival skiing. Even the sounds of my skis seemed distorted, like a record played at too low a speed.

It wasn't until I had descended about a hundred feet that instinct took over. I had been staring at my feet for the first few turns, frustrated, and when I raised my head I took in the view: a glacial expanse of blue-veined snow falling away to reveal icicle-draped cliffs. The cliffs presented the illusion of dropping forever into the jungle. I glanced quickly over my shoulder: My tracks were tight and neat on the wide, gently rolling snowfield. I had found my rhythm. I felt almost weightless. The snow was pristine—two inches of sun-softened corn atop easily edgeable hardpack. It was the type of snow that shoots off your ski tips in raisin-size chunks and plays a hissing aria as you slide on it.

It has often been said that the greater the effort expended to make them, the sweeter the turns feel. I had traveled across the globe and hiked the better part of a week to create these turns, and when they started flowing I rode a wave of euphoria, alone on the zenith of Africa. I was sliding in the most improbable of all places, yet it felt perfectly natural. For a few moments I was the freest I have ever been, or ever will be.

Three thousand vertical feet of skiing was possible. But the snowfield I was on ended in a cliff, and I'd have to hike back to the summit in order to safely descend the mountain. If I skied too far there was also a good chance I'd be too tired to make it back up. So I stopped after a short run, returned to the top, rested, then skied some more. On my third run I launched full-speed off a roll in the glacier. For an instant, as my skis scissored in the light, oxygen-starved air—champagne air!—and my stomach floated into my ribcage, I thought I'd finally trumped gravity and might never come down. I swear I floated an extra second or two.

This time, when I clambered back to the top, Chris warned me that we had a long hike down, and the nearest source of water was hours away. So we began the enormous descent, hiking as clouds gathered and the sky turned dark, hiking as snow started to fall and then, as we got lower, hiking in the rain. We camped at the first stream we saw. In the morning I limped out of the tent, legs like concrete, and scanned the summit with my binoculars. It had snowed several inches overnight, and any trace of my tracks was already gone.

Runaway Fever

One recent November, just after Thanksgiving, my friend Anne and I were driving west on Interstate 70, heading from Denver to Vail. We were on a leisurely long-distance road trip and had no intention of breaking any laws. We weren't even traveling above the speed limit. Then, 40 miles outside of Vail, we passed through the Eisenhower Tunnel at the top of Loveland Pass and our lawful intentions swiftly changed. Just past the tunnel, down the steepest part of the pass, Anne tapped me on my arm and pointed toward the highway's shoulder. "Look at that," she said.

Anne was pointing at a runaway-truck ramp. We were not, I should emphasize, in any way, shape, or form in a runaway situation. That possibility didn't even exist: The truck we were in, my small, trusty Toyota pickup, lacks the necessary tonnage and general *oomph* to achieve anything so virile as "runaway." Also, the brakes are excellent. Truth is, runaway ramps play no practical purpose in my life.

Nonetheless, I have long been fascinated with them. A ramp's aesthetic virtues are undeniable: a swoopingly graceful, exquisitely manicured, ski-jump-style arc planted like a giant nose aside the highway, free for my viewing pleasure. Truck ramps are, I believe, the closest thing we have (with the possible exception of four-leaf-clover exit arrangements) to interstate art. And their symbolism is equally satisfying: The presence of runaway ramps, which are located only on mountainous stretches of roadway, usually means ski areas are afoot.

But it was for none of these reasons that Anne was calling my attention to this particular runaway-truck ramp. This ramp she pointed to was in all ways the same as any other truck ramp after a winter snowstorm—smoothly sloped, neatly snow-covered, clearly road-signed—but with one small though profound difference. This truck ramp, unlike any truck ramp I'd seen before, had three neat sets of ski tracks snaking their way elegantly down it.

In all my years of driving to and from the ski areas of the West, after passing by hundreds, perhaps thousands, of truck ramps, the notion of runaway-ramp skiing had never once crossed my mind. The idea was so wonderfully simple, so perfectly juvenile, so sweetly humorous that I wished it were my own. But it wasn't. The skier or, more likely, skiers who had created these tracks were nowhere in sight, but their delicious turns—gleaming diamondlike in the afternoon sun, winking conspicuously at an audience of passing motorists—sent my mind reeling. My beloved runaway-truck ramps, all of a sudden, weren't merely runaway-truck ramps anymore. They were now potential ski runs.

As I drove past the skied-upon ramp, reveling in the masterful work of fellow foolish-stunt skiers, a number of significant thoughts flashed through my mind. Four, to be exact. The first: "That's brilliant!" The second: "I want to ski a truck ramp, too." The third: "But it must be illegal." The fourth: "I don't care."

Three days later, after a surprise November storm dumped 30 inches upon the Vail Valley, Anne and I returned. We drove the tunnel eastbound, exited the highway, then headed back west. We were prepared for blitzkrieg action: Anne, in the passenger seat, already had her ski boots on. Mine were waiting unbuckled and open in the back of the pickup. The rest of our gear was precisely arranged, ready for a grab-and-go. We drove through the arched exit of the tunnel, hugging the right-hand shoulder, one wheel in the breakdown lane, both of us buzzing with anticipatory nervousness. In an instant, the ramp was in front of us, its former tracks buried under a thick blanket of snow. We passed beneath a highway sign: RUNAWAY VEHICLES ONLY. The ramp was a hundred yards away. We looked for a safe spot to stash our vehicle.

I have learned, over a career based on less-than-sensical ski stunts, that no matter how well planned a mission is, there will always be an unanticipated snafu. Always. It's part of the business. Ramp skiing was no exception. Both Anne and I had remembered there being a safe, wide shoulder near the truck ramp where we could park the pickup and walk to the ramp. Neither of us, however, recalled the half dozen prominently placed NO PARKING signs fronting the ramp. And neither of us realized that all the new snow would be plowed onto the shoulder, rendering it virtually parking-proof anyway. Short of actually driving up the ramp, there was no place to stop.

Fortunately for us, there were four runaway ramps on the pass. So we headed for the next one. Once again, no safe place to stop. The third and fourth ramps—same story. We were crushed. It looked as if ramp skiing would have to wait another time, perhaps another season. Then, just as we were heading back to Vail, Anne noticed a dirt mainte-nance road winding its way behind the rocky hill upon which the final ramp was built. A lucky break. We got off at the next exit.

Ten minutes later, after a bit of wandering, we parked at the end of the dirt road. We grabbed our gear, hiked over a small knoll, and—*voilà!*—were atop the ramp. I lay down my skis and stepped in. Anne, camera in hand, moved into position to capture the stunt on film. I pointed my skis downhill, ready to ride. Rectangular road signs marked the sides of the ramp, playing the part of a ski run's evergreens. The back of the signs, not meant for public viewing, were silver-colored; the fronts were painted in bold diagonal stripes of yellow and black. The ski conditions were pristine: a foot of Colorado's finest atop a bed of groomed gravel. Four hundred feet long, intermediately sloped. Far below, four lanes of traffic sped blithely by.

The moment I was going to ski, a police car came tearing down the highway, heading toward the ramp, blue lights blazing. Our giddy grins vanished. Busted already. Instinctively, we crouched low, each trying to hide behind the other. I contemplated crawling back to the car with Anne and making a run for it. The cop flew past. We weren't the culprits. I stood up, exhaled a breath-cloud of relief, and shoved off.

It was a surprisingly difficult descent. The ramp was too flat at the top, and I had to force my ski tails around in an ugly hula-hoopish motion to complete each arc. Then, when the ramp's pitch increased and I had gained momentum, I tended to edge too hard and, two or three times, managed to create nasty-sounding scrapes as my skis bottomed out and hit raw gravel. My concentration was off, and no wonder— my primary thought as I descended the ramp was an unpleasant one: *What would happen to me if a real runaway truck decided to use this ramp right now?*

The bottom came quickly—12, maybe 14 turns—and when I glanced back my tracks looked shoddy. Not what I had in mind for my truck-ramp debut. Nevermind the cops—I needed to climb up and ski the ramp again. So I did. Much better the second time, almost good. I felt pleasurably outlawish. So I skied it once more. And then, suddenly addicted, again and again and again. Ten runs in all, until the thing practically had bumps on it and I was about to keel over from exhaustion.

Then Anne, who had been busy snapping photos during my runs, handed me the camera and took her own run. As she was heading down, an 18-wheeler repeatedly honked its air horn, giving us both third-degree goose bumps. Several dozen other semis had passed without incident, and we couldn't tell if these honks were supportive or irate. They sounded irate. We agreed it was time to make our getaway.

The whole way back to Vail, flushed with post-stunt dementia, we made firm plans to ski every truck ramp in the United States. Over the next week, however, as we finished our road trip, we passed at least 10 more skiable ramps, but the mood was never right. One ramp ski, Anne and I agreed, was enough for a lifetime.

Still, I had one last bit of unfinished business. When we returned home, I made a phone call to the Colorado State Patrol. I said I was curious about the laws, if any, governing truck-ramp skiing. The officer I was transferred to leafed through his books for several minutes before finding the correct statute. Such activity, I was told, falls under the category "Illegal Use or Obstructed Runaway Vehicle Ramp." The fine: $112, three points on your license.

The Other Side of Crazy

Nothing in the Lower 48—not the precipices of Squaw, not the chutes of Jackson, not the steeps of Stowe—has prepared me for the sight I encounter driving south on Alaska's Richardson Highway, heading toward the port city of Valdez. Here, just after the road begins its long climb toward Thompson Pass, the broad, fertile Matanushka Valley abruptly pinches shut, the horizon turns jagged, and the famed Chugach Mountains vault skyward.

In all my previous alpine experiences the mountains were shaped roughly like pyramids: broad at the base, tapering to a peak. The Chugach have dispensed with the preamble. They hardly taper. They are all peak—three-, four-, five-thousand-foot-high fangs, nearly vertical from all aspects, angled with black slate ridges. Crevassed. Treeless. Stunning.

The truly unusual part, however, is not the shape of the mountains. Fang-shaped peaks exist elsewhere in the world—Nepal, Chile, Antarctica. I have seen photos. But nowhere else on the planet can you look upward at mountains such as these, look up at rock-streaked couloirs with the approximate pitch of the Washington Monument, and see line after line of ski and snowboard tracks.

I have come here with my snowboard. I'm not as strong a snowboarder as I am a skier, but the people I've been invited to join—photographer Eric Berger and professional riders Omar Lunde, Ross Rebagliati, and a woman named Athena who has dispensed with her surname—are all top-shelf snowboarders, sponsored by various and sundry companies, and I thought it might be polite to fit in equipmentwise, if not exactly skillwise.

My group, it turns out, is standing on the side of the road, waving their thumbs. They had arrived this morning, and now, at 8:30 P.M., in the flushed arctic twilight, they've finished riding for the day. There are no chairlifts in the Chugach. The runs are reached, in increasing order of expense, by foot, by snow cat, by airplane, or, for the marquee descents, by helicopter. My group had used a helicopter. They wear expressions on their faces that suggest the early stages of shock.

I ferry the group to our headquarters—a pair of Fleetwood motor homes each the length of a city block, complete with kitchen, bedroom, and an electric step that automatically extends each time you open the door. The RVs are painted rotten-apple brown and are trimmed with bands of pink and teal, like ski sweaters from the '70s. Eric had rented them in Anchorage. They are stationed in what is officially known as the Alaska West Air parking lot but is widely referred to as the Ghetto.

The Ghetto is one of two mud-and-gravel patches that house all the services for skiing or snowboarding the Chugach. The other is the Tsaina Lodge parking lot, four miles to the north. Thompson Pass is no threat to St. Moritz. The nearest hotel is 30 miles away, in Valdez. The Ghetto is composed of a scattered collection of mobile homes, recreational vehicles, beater pickup trucks, pup tents, and mufflerless vans reeking of dope. Tucked in back is a white-and-red Bell Long Ranger helicopter and a 1954 DeHavilland Beaver. There are barbecues and lawn chairs and Frisbees and a pair of portable toilets. Several guys are standing in a circle playing hackey sack. Two people are shooting BB guns at the portable toilets. Some attempt to form groups for the next day's helicopter rides. Others try to scam rides by telling Eric they're good enough to be photographed. They'll ride anything, they say. Anything. They are junkies.

I can't blame them. Despite heavy coverage from filmmakers and magazine writers, the Chugach Mountains still represent the last great frontier of North American skiing and snowboarding. Most mountains in the area haven't yet been tracked. Entire subranges haven't even been named. First-ever descents are a daily occurrence.

Helicopter skiing did not begin here until 1990, when, in the wake of the disastrous Valdez oil spill, the region was seeking sources of revenue that didn't rely on healthy runs of fish. The next year, the World Extreme Skiing Championship was established, and soon every brand-name rider and skier in America made a visit. Word got around: bottomless snow, ridiculous steeps, no rules. Pilgrims began arriving. Some weren't as good as they thought they were. A few died.

Now the area is slowly maturing. The helicopter services have recently decided to make guides mandatory. Even so, no matter how skilled you are, if you're seeking to push your limits, the Chugach is the place to be.

In the morning, I put on my climbing harness and my avalanche transceiver. I pack my shovel, ice ax, and first-aid kit. Eric has hired the services of H_2O Heli Adventures, one of the region's three flying and guiding operations. Our guide is veteran Chugach rider Dan Caruso. The sky is a cloudless, wet-paint blue. Eighteen inches of snow have fallen in the past week. We are going where no one has touched it, to a remote area called the Books.

Through the bubble of the helicopter I have a front-row view of a dozen glaciers, choppy and cracked and melded with the flanks of the mountains. Glaciers may move only a few inches a year but the impression they prompt is of raw, tumbling speed. Sheer slate walls, thousands of feet of opaque rock, rise vertically from the ice. Impossible-seeming cornices jut off windblown summits like the bills of baseball caps. I grasp a new understanding of the term knife-edge ridge. I see no place to land.

For all practical purposes, there isn't. Snowboarding the Chugach, though, is hardly practical. Picking a run is a seat-of-the-pants proposition. The guide looks out the window, spots a good face to ride, then asks the pilot if it's possible to put the helicopter down atop it. We hover over one spot, then another—the ridges are too narrow, too unstable. On our third attempt, we land on a dome of snow no bigger than a pitcher's mound. Gingerly, the six of us exit the chopper and unload our boards. We huddle together. The machine flies away.

From our perch, I can see an uncountable array of peaks. What I can't see, however, is the mountain I'm standing on. In all directions, the slope drops off below my field of vision. It is as if we've landed on a cloud. I feel dizzy. Though it's well below freezing, I begin to sweat. Eric straps on his board and shuffles to the south-facing slope. He peers over, and drops off. Then Omar, then Athena, then Ross.

"How steep is this?" I ask Dan.

"Not very. Forty-five, maybe fifty degrees." Then he disappears, too.

I crawl over to the edge. The slope is so steep it does not seem possible snow could stick to it. Most places it wouldn't. The rare combination of low-elevation peaks, proximity to the sea, surplus of snowfall, and extreme midwinter cold has resulted in a phenomenon whereby snow clings to virtually any surface in the Chugach, no matter the pitch. And only rarely does it avalanche.

My first turn is shaky. I traverse onto the slope on my toe-side. While standing upright on my board, I can extend my hand and touch the hill in front of me. This is a new category of steep. For the Chugach, it isn't even a difficult run. I flex my knees, uncoil, and flip onto my heelside. Then, unaccustomed to the steepness, I sit down on the slope. The top six inches of snow slides from beneath my board, exposing a layer that glints in the sun like glass. Everyone else has managed to miss it, but I've found the ice.

I quickly stand up and hop back to my toeside, but this is a mistake—more ice is exposed. It's all around me now. I start to slip.

"Turn!" Dan yells, watching me from below.

But it is too late. My edge loses its bite, and I fall. Ten feet. Twenty. I paw at the slope with my gloves but there's nothing to grab. For a few seconds, my heart does not beat. I think: That's it. I have fallen on a run where falling is not allowed.

Then I stop. Falling, it turns out, is allowed. The ice slick was 30 feet long, and it shot me directly into a winddrift of powder. I'm suddenly thigh-deep in snow.

"Well, you've found the sweet spot," says Dan. He's grinning. "Rip it up."

I rest for a few moments, letting my panic fade. I convince myself that I'd merely been unlucky. I'd done nothing wrong. I start to ride.

In my relatively brief snowboarding career, I have experienced some premium powder in some world-famous places. But here, in Alaska, this early May snow I've nearly killed myself getting to is far and away the finest. My board cuts three-foot furrows, spindrift swirling about me, catching the sun. Everything is silent. The snow is light as down. I don't so much ride as float. I ease out slow, rounded arcs—safe, savoring. My rhythm feels hypnotic. The run is 4,000 vertical feet.

After two more runs and no more ice, we return to the Ghetto and unwind. We tell stories about the powder to the others in the parking lot. In the morning, though, reality strikes: I get the bill. The price is steeper than the terrain—my three runs cost $331. This is beyond the means of most people who are not regularly pictured in *Forbes,* so I decide to spend my second day doing things the cheap way. I'm going to hike.

Finding a partner is simple—the Ghetto houses no shortage of the dedicated but destitute. His name is Chris, a boarder from Massachusetts who is spending the winter in Valdez, eating peanut-butter sandwiches ("Can't afford jelly."), camping out ("Can't afford hotels."), and hiking the mountains ("Can't afford helicopters."). We drive down the pass in Chris's Westphalia, looking at possible road runs. There are thousands of them. We choose an obvious one: a large chute, wide as the highway, cupped between two rocky foothills a short slog from the road. If this run were anywhere near my hometown there would be 200 people scrambling up it every weekend. The thing would be a mogul field. But we are in Alaska. The chute is untracked.

The climb takes two hours. With my board slung across my back, I kick steps up the left edge of the chute. Kick, stop, breathe. Kick, stop, breathe. I hum to myself. Sometimes, when I stray too close to the rock wall lining the chute, I encounter a patch of rotten snow and sink to my hip. Within half an hour, I'm down to my T-shirt. Every now and then a helicopter swoops across the sky, but I'm not jealous. I'm earning my turns. I feel superior.

Two bald eagles soar overhead—it's mating season, and the Valdez area is practically congested with eagles. All along the road they perch on the top of black spruces, transmitting wide-eyed, challenging stares. When one launches, it is a soundless explosion of energy. The tree shakes for nearly a minute. The pair above me ride the updrafts, circling higher and higher in the brilliant sky until they disappear. Not once do they flap. Now I'm jealous.

At the top of the chute, there is a patch of burgundy wildflowers and a rusty shotgun shell. I sniff the flowers, pocket the shell, and strap on my board. The temperature at the lower elevations has been too warm to preserve the powder, but the snow has congealed into smooth spring corn. I ride the couloir without stopping, leaning into the turns with exaggerated body movements, arms outstretched, wind rippling through my hair, inscribing a broad helix the length and breadth of the couloir. Chris does the same. I'd like to think the eagles were impressed.

Back at the Ghetto there is a group of riders sitting in white plastic lawn chairs, finishing a Doritos and 7Up lunch, and pointing at the mountains, talking big behind their Oakleys.

"How about the south side of New World?"

"No way, man. Got tracks on it."

"Main line off Cold Smoke?"

"Been there, done that."

"West face of Python?"

"That's an idea."

An airplane ride is swiftly organized. The DeHavilland Beaver seats eight; there's a couple of spots available. Thirty-five bucks a ride. What the hell? I jump in. The engine clatters to life. The pilot, whose name is Tom, makes an announcement: "There's no movie on this flight, but if any of you care to step onto the wing, I'll show you *Gone with the Wind*." We rumble down the packed-snow runway.

Five minutes later we land on a flat glacier 3,000 feet above the Ghetto. It's late in the afternoon and the sun is dropping behind the Worthington Glacier, across the valley, causing the ice to glow as if lit from within. I ride and ride and ride, the fattest turns possible, turns that would gobble up an entire Vail back bowl with a single arc, and still I don't cross another track. I feel like the ultimate powder pig. I love it. The run returns me to the road, where I flash my thumb and catch a ride home.

The next day, I turn the tables again. Once more, I decide not to join Eric and the pros. Instead, I drive to the Tsaina Lodge and book a day with Valdez Heli-Ski Guides, the company owned by husband-and-wife extreme skiers Doug Coombs and Emily Gladstone. Their service is reputed to offer the best access to the Chugach's wildest descents. It is not cheap. A six-run day costs $450. The waiver I'm given includes a detailed questionnaire:

Are you comfortable on 45-degree slopes?

This is steeper than virtually every lift-served run in the United States. "Yes," I write.

Fifty-five degrees?

This is so steep you'd have to climb up it with crampons and an ice ax. I have never ridden a 55-degree slope. But I'm feeling confident. "Yes," I write.

Sixty?

This is practically an elevator shaft. "Yes."

I am paired with four alarmingly adrenalized Chugach fanatics, including our guide, a lanky, bushy-bearded Montanan named Jerry Hance. There is another snowboarder, also named Mike, who'd come from southern

California to spend a month here. The other two skiers are Jade, from Hawaii, and Jeff, a Taos ski instructor. We ride a snappy A-Star chopper into the mountains, flying over a network of bear tracks and a pair of mountain goats clinging to a thin ledge, before landing on a ledge of our own. The first run is disappointing, a short shot on wind-crusted snow.

The second run is the scariest experience of my life. The pilot, a middle-aged, gray-haired man named Walt who initially appeared to be the very essence of sanity, turns out to be the helicopter version of Evel Knievel. He hovers above a summit knob that doesn't contain enough real estate to plant a phone booth. One half of one runner is touching snow when we're given the exit signal. We leap from the chopper and grab hold of an outcropping of rocks until Walt flies away.

I stand up, then instantly squat back down. The first run of the trip, when I'd slipped on the ice, was merely terrifying. This is something else entirely.

"This is extreme," says Jerry. Everyone but me seems thrilled.

We are on a run called Flatiron, which is anything but flat. It has not been descended in four years. This is understandable. Save for one narrow ribbon of snow, the summit ridge drops off into vertical cliffs. Extreme—you fall, you die. Simple as that. My breathing becomes labored. *This is beyond crazy*, I think. *This is stupid.*

"Watch for hidden ice," says Jerry.

I think about my previous encounter with ice. "What if I find it?"

"Don't," says Jerry. "Don't."

Once again, I let everyone else go first. I try to focus. If this section of the run were at a ski area, without the cliffs, I'd ride it no problem. But now that the penalty for a mistake is my life, I can't move. So I swallow my pride, put my hands on the ground and gingerly sideslip down the ribbon, obliterating everyone else's neat tracks, to where the group has gathered overlooking the main face of Flatiron. I look down.

It's about 60 degrees. Crevassed in a series of broad frowns. Peppered with loose rock. Wide, though. We stand silently for a moment, gathering confidence. On a nearby peak a few boulders, loosened by the intense sunlight, clatter down a cliff. Echoes rumble up from the valley floor.

I ride the run. Not well, not smoothly, but I ride. I am focused so intensely on my turns there is not a single extraneous thought in my head. My whole world is the next carve. Extreme riding, I realize, is meditation for madmen. The run is so steep the top three inches of snow peel away and slide down with me. The sensation is of riding over a waterfall. I can't look at my feet. And I can't look at the horizon: I am on the steepest pitch imaginable and the run *still* rolls away beneath me. So I ride in my own focused bubble, one careful turn at a time.

I ride 5,000 vertical feet before my concentration breaks. Then I nearly die. At the bottom of Flatiron, running completely across the slope, is a narrow crevasse, called a bergschrund, where the valley glacier has peeled away from the mountain. Jerry's instructions, insane as they sound, are to gather up speed and jump across the bergschrund. After that the run would essentially be over, and we could ride freely to the helicopter's landing zone.

From my final stopping point, the bergschrund looks no more than a foot wide. A foot—easy. So I do not gain much speed. I approach the crack almost leisurely. It is not until I am right at the lip that I realize my miscalculation. The bergschrund is not one foot wide. It is not two or three. It is five feet wide. At the last instant, I instinctively yank my front foot upward and launch myself forward. I look directly into the center of the Earth. It is a luminescent pit of jade-blue ice. Bottomless. They won't even bother to retrieve my body.

I land with the front half of my board on the snow, the rear half hanging over the abyss. I tumble forward, flip once, twice, three times, and slide face first on the cold, wet snow.

I consider quitting for the day, but Jerry promises we won't be doing anything that intense again. So I stay for the final four runs. Though all are far harder than anything I'd ever ridden in the Lower 48, they are a comparative breeze. We even complete a first-ever descent, which I'm allowed to name. The run is short and feisty, so I call it Napoleon. We ride Napoleon twice, waist-deep in snow on a slope that's waited all eternity to be carved, leaving behind tracks befitting the honor. I begin to feel comfortable with the terrain.

Odd as this seems, by the time we've flown back to the Tsaina Lodge, instead of savoring my safe return I find that I'm nearly ready to push myself again.

So I hang out in the parking lot. And sure enough, just before sunset, there's talk of skiing the north face of Diamond Peak. Diamond is one of the Chugach's premier shots: a vertical mile of unending steepness. A helicopter needs to be filled, pronto. The excitement in the Tsaina Lodge parking lot is palpable. People are buzzing on adrenaline. It's contagious; I'm susceptible. I stand on a rock and look up at the peak, lit in salmon-tinted light by the waning sun. Gorgeous.

Jade comes over. "Five thousand more vertical," he says. "The conditions are pristine."

I'm tempted. I can't help it. "Is there some exposure?" I ask.

"Some."

"How much is some?"

"Well, there's a few no-fall turns."

"Oh."

"Flatiron was all no-fall turns. You'll be half as scared this time. You'll see."

I stare over the roof of the Tsaina, over the spruces, up at Diamond Peak. It is a painful decision. "I don't think I'm a good enough snowboarder yet," I say.

"Well," Jade says to me tersely, "at least you know your limits."

Then he leaves to find someone else willing to ride. This is Valdez—his task is easy. The helicopter soon departs, and I'm alone in the parking lot. The brave are flying to the mountain, the meek are at the bar. I want to be up there, I think, with the pioneers, adventuring, challenging myself, *living*. But overriding all my machismo is a basic truth: I don't want to die.

Carving the Toothbrush

As the Brits would say, I burned my bum. Badly. The left side of my gluteus felt as if it had been dipped in a deep fryer, and when I went into the base lodge and peeked in my ski pants, I saw a bruise the size of a softball materializing on my upper thigh.

Granted, I had been warned. "Beware of bee stings, burns, and breaking your thumb, aye?" the woman at the lift-ticket booth had said to me, correctly assuming from my American accent that I'd never skied in Scotland before. "And take it slow. Skiing the toothbrush ain't as easy as she looks."

And admittedly, it did appear easy. Odd, but easy. The toothbrush, which is also called the mat or the plastic, is what dedicated skiers in Great Britain are often forced to slide upon. Britain, severely shortchanged when the Alps were distributed, does have a few snow-skiing areas, but snowfall is sparse and temperatures are often too warm to make artificial snow. Plastic offers Britain's only reliable form of skiing. The surface is a series of inch-and-a-half-high white PVC bristles arranged in a diamond-shaped pattern, like a chain-link fence, with each diamond about a palm's width across. Small clumps of grass poke through the grid. The slopes, unnaturally white against a lush green background, look like a conceptual art installation inspired by Christo. Toothbrush skiers use the same gear as snow skiers, and the technique is roughly the same as well. The main difference is that snow is a relatively low-friction surface while the plastic burns your bum.

But singed seat or no, I wasn't going to take it slow. I had not flown all the way across the Atlantic just to leisurely ski down the toothbrush. I came to *race*. As the only American entered in the British Dry Ski Slopes Championships, I single-handedly carried the hopes and dreams of an entire nation. This was, in many ways, an ambassadorial ski mission. And I had more than one cheek to give for my country.

Great Britain's snow-skiing team, as anyone who follows World Cup racing knows, is skiing's equivalent of the Washington Generals. But on the plastic, the Brits are untouchable. Of the 100 dry slopes in Europe, 90 of them are in the U.K.; the others are in Holland and Ireland. And the one I was racing at—Hillend Ski Centre, in the Pentland

Hills just south of Edinburgh—is the longest toothbrush on Earth, more than a quarter mile from end to end, with a vertical drop of about 350 feet. It's not exactly Chamonix, but Hillend does have a lengthier season—it's open 52 weeks a year. And if the mat were any longer, the friction created by the bristles would cause ski bases to melt. As it is, a ski lasts only a few months on the plastic before its base must be replaced. The rental shop at Hillend resoles each of its 2,500 pairs four times a year.

The Dry Slopes Championships were scheduled for two days; slalom the first, giant-slalom the second. I arrived the morning of the slalom. It was a warm September day, 70 degrees out, with not a millimeter of snow in sight. There were 208 competitors, ranging in age from 18 to 33 and representing men's and women's teams from Scotland, England, and Wales, along with contingents from Holland and Ireland. Nearly everyone was feverishly at work filing and waxing and buffing their skis. This race is serious: Most members of the British Olympic team are champion toothbrush racers, and coaches from the national squad were at Hillend, scouting for future talent. The championships is also one of the few times these racers get to compete in front of a home audience—British snow-skiing events are held at major resorts on mainland Europe. The Dry Slopes Championships, which have been held annually since 1970, are by far the most prestigious ski races contested on British soil.

After a good deal of finagling, I had received special permission from the British Ski Federation to participate in the championships. The other competitors had qualified after a series of elimination races. I wanted to perform well, so instead of socializing with my fellow competitors, I gathered up my gear and headed to the slopes for a few practice runs. Trail maps are not required at Hillend. The area consists of three base buildings (restaurant, lodge, rental shop), three runs (Tow Slope, Main Slope, Nursery Slope), and three lifts (T-bar, poma, double chair). I boarded the double, but not before shuffling through the waxing tent, in which an automated contraption applies a thin coat of wax to the bottom of your skis while you're still wearing them. Waxing before each run, I was told, is essential for maximum plastic performance. The syrupy odor of melted wax hangs thick in Hillend's air. Most racers, in order to further enhance slideability, also add their own home-brewed concoction to their bases. Products I witnessed being used for this purpose included furniture polish, shaving cream, dish-washing liquid, vegetable oil, deodorant spray, and leather buffer.

My chair ride to Hillend's 1,100-foot summit was unusual. In the fields alongside the slopes I watched hundreds of sheep gorging themselves on the rich grass of the Pentlands. On the rolling fairways near the base area, golfers paraded about in their plaids. Behind me was the gabled skyline of downtown Edinburgh, and behind that the dark waters of the Firth of Forth. Beneath my skis were patches of violet-colored willow herbs, humming with bees. And floating in the air were small clouds of pollen spores—enough, sometimes, so that it almost appeared to be snowing.

The slopes were packed. Racers were warming up, lessons were being taught, season-pass holders were making their morning turns. The British, it turns out, have taken dedication to the sport of skiing to a whole new level. Many of them have spent a lifetime skiing and have never made a single turn on snow. On my first ride up, my chairmate was a 12-year-old Irish racer named Ciaran Lee. Ciaran told me he has skied 50 days a year since he was five and hasn't even *seen* snow.

Hillend has been open since 1964. It is financially subsidized by the city of Edinburgh, and receives more than 150,000 skier visits a year. These are skiers who have, by necessity, developed fine senses of humor. One winter, in an attempt to make things appear more snowlike, Hillend tried baking soda as a ski surface. It gummed up like porridge. Another time, during a base-lodge barbecue, the slopes caught fire. They had to be replaced. The closest Hillend ever gets to a snowstorm is a good, firm frost—when that happens the place is jammed as if it were a powder day.

But despite runs that have all the pitch of a dinner plate, the skiing at Hillend is fiendishly difficult. When I first got off the chair, I found myself unable to turn. I skied straight off the side of the mat and onto the grass. I crawled back to the plastic and snowplowed for a minute, getting a feel for the toothbrush. Then I bore down hard, weighting my skis as if I were in two feet of slop. I managed to carve a few turns, in a way. Plastic is even more unforgiving than ice—every flaw in your technique is highlighted. My main problem is that I sit too far back on my skis. And on my third warm-up run, just as I'd gotten up to half-decent speed and was almost feeling confident, this problem manifested itself with an improperly weighted edge set followed by a 30-foot plastic-bristle butt slide.

Toothbrush falls are legendary among British skiers. Everyone has a story. Catching a thumb under the mat is so prevalent that British medical books refer to a certain break as a Hillend Thumb. Fully one fifth of the racers at the championships possessed dry-slope skiing's badge of honor: a hand encased in plaster. (A wrist-length cast, even two, does not seem to prevent anyone from competing.) Burns can be worse than breaks. A vicious fall can not only leave permanent scars but also destroy a ski outfit. Most racers were wearing helmets, knee pads, and specially padded pants.

My fall was relatively minor, though remarkably painful. I limped into the lodge. The best cure, I decided, was a pre-race snack. The special of the day at the café was haggis. Haggis is a sheep's stomach stuffed with its minced heart, lungs, and liver. It is a Scottish delicacy. This was served with tatties (boiled potatoes) and neeps (stewed turnips). The texture and odor of haggis, at least to me, brought to mind a certain brand of expensive dog food. I ate it anyway, and it did not sit well. The pain in my rear shifted to my stomach. I popped two Advils and went back up the hill to the start of the race.

The slalom course stretched from the top of Hillend to the bottom, and was tight and narrow, designed to favor technique masters who could carve on plastic rather than speed demons who didn't care about melting their skin. My plan for American victory was to learn the secret of dry-slope racing by watching the other competitors. This did not happen. The race directors decided that since I was the only entrant not part of a team, I would be the first racer.

The starter gave me a three count, and I kicked out of the starting gate fast. Too fast. I had waded through the auto waxer four times before the run, and gates flew at me like bats out of a cave. My hands, flailing to maintain balance, pantomimed a series of semaphore signals. I grimaced; I grunted; I spat; I swore. A pole smacked me directly on my butt bruise. My skis, scraping against the plastic, created an unnatural sound, like two large pieces of Velcro being pulled apart.

I managed to ride the course out with no disqualifiable errors. My time was just over 30 seconds. Being the first racer, I was now in first place. Hope springs eternal, so I hung around the finish area to see if my time would hold up. Hope lasted 26.8 seconds. And 15 racers later, I was already down to 13th place. My bum began to throb.

I wandered into the cafeteria, where a postrace party was already starting to gather steam. Scotland may have artificial skiing, but the après part is the real thing. And as soon as some of the race directors spotted the Yank, as I'd been forcibly nicknamed, I was encouraged to drink "a wee dram" of Scotch. I was handed a damn big dram of Dalwhinnie 15-year-old single malt. Neat. It was sweet and peaty and down-right delicious. By the time I was halfway through the glass my bum felt perfectly fine.

Small and Smaller

When I asked Bob Enzel my question, there was a long pause on the other end of the line. A throat was cleared. "You're serious?" he said. I told him I was. Enzel, who publishes *The White Book of Ski Areas,* an annually updated listing of virtually every ski hill in North America, has undoubtedly stockpiled more data on more ski destinations than any other person in the U.S. And last season, after reading for the umpteenth year each ski magazine's roster of the grandest, most ostentatious, most overhyped resorts, I realized that I was weary of the whole biggest-best thing. I wanted to know what was the tiniest, most vertically challenged, least significant ski pimple in America. And I wanted to spend a day skiing there. So I called Enzel.

Finding the littlest ski area in the United States, it turned out, was an Aspen-size undertaking. Enzel studied vertical drops (smallest); he examined skiable acres (fewest); he investigated lift capacities (least); length of runs (shortest); and snowmaking systems (most primitive). His computers buzzed and whirred. And when the disk drives ceased, it was discovered that Paul Bunyan, Wisconsin, was small; Frost Ridge, New York, was minuscule; Mount McSauba, Michigan, was microscopic; but the champion, the lowest of the low, the Smallest Ski Area in America, was a place near Syracuse, New York, called Four Seasons Ski Center.

I flew from my home in the powder-rich Rockies to the brown hummocks of upstate New York. I rented a car and drove east from Syracuse, through farmlands swiftly being encroached upon by suburbia. Fifteen minutes outside the city, a swatch of snow materialized on the right—it appeared and vanished as quickly a camera flash—and before I had a chance to think, *That's it!* I had driven right by. I pulled a U-turn and joined two dozen other cars in the muddy parking lot of Four Seasons Ski Center.

Inside the ranch-house-style base lodge I was greeted with an impressive noise. It was school vacation week in Syracuse, and a large herd of kinetic preteens seemed to be in the process of a coup d'état, running from the rental shop to the pinball machine to the snack bar, pieces of munchkin ski gear strewn in their wake. Most of the parents had enrolled their kids in Four Seasons' learn-to-ski program and, wisely, had headed off to run errands. A sign on the bathroom door encapsulated the clientele's level of ski savvy: ATTENTION SKIERS! PLEASE DO NOT WEAR SKIS INTO REST ROOM.

Four Seasons' owner, John Goodfellow, was in the midst of this bedlam, attempting to direct traffic. Goodfellow—tall, soft-spoken, cardigan-sweatered—bore a striking resemblance to Mr. Rogers, patriarch of PBS's happy neighborhood. Goodfellow is 48 years old and has run Four Seasons for 25 years. His father ran it before him. "I taught the parents of some of these kids how to ski," he said as he rounded everyone up and got them out the door. Goodfellow has two other full-time employees, Phil and Bill, and receives fewer than 3,000 skier visits a year. Money is tight. The area doubles as a driving range during the summer (hence its name), but other attempts to generate additional income have been a disaster—the restaurant burned down, the tennis bubble collapsed. Paying the insurance bill is often a struggle. But at least Four Seasons is alive. According to Enzel, more than 600 U.S. ski areas—50 percent of all hills—have gone out of business in the past 15 years.

When I informed Goodfellow that his area was selected as the nation's smallest, he seemed genuinely honored ("Who would want to be second smallest?"), but he didn't think the title would help business. "People walk in here all the time," he explained, "and say, 'Where's the rest of your hill?' I say, 'That's it.' They say, 'Where's your chairlift?' I say, 'We don't have one.' Then they usually leave."

I elected to stay. A day at Four Seasons costs $12; a season pass is $75. The area is only open weekends and holidays. A good winter has 30 ski days; a lousy year, less than a dozen. About 10 season passes are sold annually. Four Seasons relies entirely on natural snow—the electricity bills generated by snowguns would put it permanently in the red. There's also no night skiing. And to ensure the area will always be struggling for business, no snowboarding is allowed, either.

The absence of snowguns was apparent as I stepped out the lodge's back door and examined the slopes. Make that singular: slope. Four Seasons claims four trails, 100 feet of vertical, and 12 skiable acres, but even these modest numbers seem highly inflated. The place has two lifts, a J-bar and a rope tow, both serving one diminutive ridge, at the top of which sits the Changing Seasons housing development. The skiable terrain is entirely gentle and mostly treeless, except for a small section to the skiers' left—what is referred to as the intermediate and expert area—where you can wind through a stand of maples. The snow depth at the summit was about four inches. In spots, it had drifted to as much as half a foot. In other spots, you could build a mud castle. Fortunately, Four Seasons is endowed with such smooth and rock-free grass that the ski area can be fully operational with a base of less than two inches.

In front of the J-bar loading area was a second scene of unmitigated chaos. The children were attempting to put on their ski equipment, most of them fumbling with their gear as though it were emitting electric shocks. I explained to four boys how a binding works. I presented an impromptu lecture on the efficacy of the ski brake. I unraveled for a small audience the mystery of the boot buckle. On the J-bar, I watched, impressed, as several new lift-riding techniques were tested, including the popular I-won't-let-go-even-though-my-face-is-furrowing-the-snow uphill body drag.

The line for the J-bar, the only lift that goes to the top (the rope tow peters out after about 50 feet), demanded maximal patience. Between shutdowns to rescue tangled riders and skipped bars by panicked first-timers, it took nearly 15 minutes to reach the front. During the ride to the top, I saw, out on the slope, a young boy crash into an even younger girl three separate times in about 15 feet. After the third mishap, the boy looked at the girl apologetically, and gingerly asked, "Do you hate me?" Replied the girl: "Yes, I do."

The J-bar ends a few feet shy of the living room of one of the houses in the Changing Seasons development. I studied the view from Four Seasons' summit, elevation 550: housing developments, traffic on Highway 5, snowless hills. Then I pushed off. *One Mississippi. Two Mississippi.* I was at the bottom.

After three trips on the J-bar, I asked Jeremy the lift operator if I could hike up instead of waiting on the interminable line. "No problem," he said. I shouldered my skis. Eighty-seven seconds later—I timed it—I was back on top. The runs at Four Seasons, it seems, are too short to have creative names; they're simply labeled Easier, More Difficult, and

Most Difficult. More and Most are gladed: In a way, they're like Shadows at Steamboat (granted, in the same way that a tree house is like the Taj Mahal). I followed a kid wearing a sweatshirt that said GIVE BLOOD: PLAY HOCKEY down More, and he led me right to Four Seasons' hidden jump. I *knew* there had to be a jump. Every ski area, regardless of size, has to have a jump somewhere; it's an unwritten rule. Give Blood gamely launched it, way off balance, and very nearly fulfilled his sweatshirt's first commandment. I retrieved his skis for him. Next time up, I flew down More, skidding perilously on a patch of wet leaves—damn tricky things to carve on—then flung myself off the jump and was all of a sudden in high spirits. I felt as if I were 10 years old.

I spent the afternoon hiking and skiing, giving brief pointers to pretzeled skiers, and playing with my stopwatch and altimeter. My fastest run down Four Seasons clocked in at 4.1 seconds; my slowest took just over half a minute. Average number of turns per run: nine. And when I checked the vertical drop on my altimeter, it registered—rounding up—80 feet. But it has to be the world's most amusing 80 feet of skiing. At least once a run, I witnessed a mishap so peculiar— ski caught behind head; pole lodged in tree; tongue stuck to J-bar—that I couldn't help but laugh aloud. Almost always, the victim laughed with me. This was skiing's next generation, still in the training-wheel stage. I didn't hear one person complain about the conditions or moan about the vertical or lament the absence of a chairlift. Four Seasons was paradise to these kids. In 10 years, some of these same skiers will be dominating the steeps of Alta and Whistler and Jackson Hole. But they'll never forget where they started.

Sarajevo Rising

In February of 1984, the Winter Olympics were held in the bustling, mountain-ringed city of Sarajevo, in what was then the nation of Yugoslavia. For American ski racers, it was an extraordinary Games. Phil Mahre won the slalom, a fifth of a second ahead of his identical-twin brother, Steve. Debbie Armstrong, a virtual unknown, took gold in the giant-slalom; her teammate, Christin Cooper, captured the silver.

But the most memorable performance, at least to me, was the improbable, runaway-truck run in the downhill by Bill Johnson, the wild man out of California whom the Sarajevans still refer to as "The Cowboy." I was a teenager at the time, an aspiring racer myself, and I recall taping a photo from *Sports Illustrated* to my headboard—Johnson, in his orange-and-white candycane of an outfit, a meter of air beneath his skis, arms forward, knees tucked, carrying some seriously perilous speed.

The other picture from the Sarajevo Games that earned a berth on my headboard, though for slightly more prurient reasons, was of the German figure skater Katarina Witt. Witt's sensual, balletic long program resulted not only in a gold medal but also in an estimated 30,000 love letters, none of which were sent by me, though several were composed, I'm sure, as I slipped off to sleep.

Fifteen years to the month after Johnson and Witt and the Mahres won their medals, I traveled for the first time to Sarajevo. In the period between the Olympics and my visit, the city had regressed from one of Europe's most ethnically diverse, coolly cosmopolitan places into a bombed-out memorial to the dominions of hatred and war.

Sarajevo is now the capital of Bosnia-Herzegovina, a nation that emerged from the breakup of Yugoslavia in 1991. Within Bosnia reside large populations of three distinct cultures: Serb, Croat, and Muslim. Serbs are Eastern Orthodox; Croats are Roman Catholic; and the Muslims, of course, are followers of Islam, though the version practiced in Bosnia is an informal, almost secular one, free from hardline fundamentalists. During Yugoslavia's communist era, religious nationalism was strongly suppressed. The freedoms that accompanied independence, however, also released the binds on ancient hatreds, and for nearly four years, from 1992 through 1995, the Serbs, Croats, and Muslims attempted, with considerable success, to exterminate one another.

Out of Bosnia's prewar population of five million, more than 200,000 were killed. Another 200,000 were wounded, and two million fled the country. Half of the nation's schools were destroyed, and 40 percent of the bridges. In Sarajevo alone, 2,000 children were murdered. Every Olympic facility was demolished. To heat their homes, people cut down trees in city parks, or chopped up wooden benches. The National Library was destroyed, the books scorched. Soccer fields were turned into cemeteries. All of the animals in the Sarajevo zoo starved to death.

Peace talks were finally held, in Dayton, Ohio, in September of 1995. The Dayton accords halted the war, but Bosnia is now a segregated nation. The country is divided into two entities—the Bosnian Federation, which includes Sarajevo, is home primarily to Croats and Muslims (tensions between these two groups have subsided); the Serb Republic, encompassing northern and eastern Bosnia, is populated almost exclusively by Serbs. Few people dare cross between the two. Thirty-four thousand NATO troops are enforcing the peace. As many as a half million land mines may still be buried.

I had not considered Sarajevo a viable ski destination until I received a startling press release from the Bosnian Olympic Committee. Though much of Sarajevo was still in ruins, and though fighting was intensifying in neighboring Kosovo, the committee said that Sarajevo would soon be rebuilt. They said money from relief agencies and national governments was flowing in. The ski hills, they reported, were back in operation for the first time in six years. They proclaimed their city ready to return to prominence. And then they announced that Sarajevo was officially declaring its candidacy for the 2010 Winter Olympics. A week later, I was on my way.

◆ ◆ ◆

I did not travel to Sarajevo alone. My friend Chris Anderson, who is a professional photographer, had made many trips to Sarajevo during the war, and had befriended several Sarajevans. When Chris heard of the plan to regain the Olympic Games, he phoned me. As a result of the Dayton agreements, the Olympic ski hill that had hosted the women's events was now in the Serb Republic; the mountain the men raced on, though only 20 miles away, was in the Bosnian Federation. This seemed a touchy situation. Chris and I wondered what it was like, skiing on former Olympic hills, and former battlefields, so soon after the hostilities had ended. Was it possible that the Games could actually return?

One of Chris's friends, a Bosnian Muslim named Haris Hrustemović, picked us up at the Sarajevo airport. Our fellow airline passengers, for the most part, were soldiers or relief workers. During the war, the area around the airport had suffered intense shelling—my first glimpse of Sarajevo was of a block of row houses practically minced from bombing. Those homes still standing remained upright only by leaning against one another. Most were piles of rubble. A nearby office building looked as though it had been flipped inside out, like a dirty sweatshirt, with the pipes and ducts and stairwells now on the outside. A sign, written in Bosnian and English, announced that the Swiss Federation for Mine Clearance was currently "demining this area."

A street away, though, a new housing project was complete, the units painted in a rainbow of cheery pastel hues. Here, a billboard advertised Tide laundry detergent; a neon sign over a small restaurant read PIZZA. I could see a half dozen construction cranes. A mosque was being repaired, its minarets encased in scaffolding. There was the sense, in this sudden juxtaposition, that I was witnessing a transformation of near-frenzied momentum—as swift and, it occurred to me, as superficial as a set change at the theater.

Haris took us to his apartment, a 10-minute drive from the airport, and introduced us to his wife, Sabina. They were both in their early 30s. Haris is compact and muscular, with a wrestler's physique, dark eyes, and a quiet demeanor. He is employed by a Sarajevo radio station. Sabina is thin and elegant, with long black hair and a sexy way of smoking cigarettes that reminded me of movie stars from the 1920s. She works as an accountant for a war-reparation fund. They wed during the war, and had to wait two years before they were able to take their first walk together as a married couple.

Their apartment is on the sixth floor of a 12-story tene-
ment in the Sarajevo outskirts. In the living room, two walls
were patched with plywood, where a missile had blasted
through—fortunately, neither Haris nor Sabina were home
at the time. The façade of their building, as with every building in the neighborhood, was a moonscape of mortar-shell
hits, rebar spilling from some holes like loose wiring.
Concrete slabs were constantly falling from buildings.
During the five days I was in Sarajevo, two people died after
being struck by debris.

♦ ♦ ♦

The ski area of Bjelasnica, site of the men's Olympic ski
events, is so close to Sarajevo that the start shack for the
downhill can be seen from the center of town. A cab ride to
the mountain costs the equivalent of $10. Chris and I head-
ed there early in the morning, on a warm, cloudless
Saturday, and found ourselves in a long line of cars.

Bjelasnica is an unimposing mountain, bald on top, with
broad shoulders dropping evenly into a thick spruce forest.
The main run, scene of Bill Johnson's victory, is wide open
and smooth, zigzagging from summit to base. The snow was
deep, baked by the sun into fine spring corn. Two lifts were
operating—a T-bar and a double chair, both funded by gifts
from the Austrian government—though neither ascended
more than halfway up the hill. All that remained of the
upper-mountain lifts were a few forlorn-looking towers; the
money needed for further repairs had not yet materialized.

What most caught my eye were the three base-area hotels, scenes of mass celebrations at the Games. All three were now complete wrecks, ceilings collapsed upon floors, walls dangling like broken shutters, not a pane of glass remaining. And yet despite the destruction, and the limited terrain, the area was flooded with people.

I had spent the previous day in downtown Sarajevo, visiting with several well-known Bosnian skiers. One of them, Dr. Fahrudin Kulenović, the director of the Sarajevo Institute for Public Health, the doctor for the Bosnian national ski team, and a driving force behind both the 1984 Games and the bid for the 2010 Olympics, has skied in Bosnia for 44 years. He spoke passionately about the return of skiing to Sarajevo: "I am not denying that there is poverty here, and destruction, and the scars of war, but the reopening of the ski areas is of utmost importance. It is a symbol of the recovering health of the country—of our economic health, of our physical health. We are saying that you can now escape the confines of the city, and the memories there, and once again go into the mountains. For many of us, I believe, it's a sort of therapy."

It appeared to be working. Three quarters of the people at the hill seemed to have no intention of skiing. In the large snowy meadow at the base of the mountain, there were soccer games going on, and picnics, and snow sculpting. Children ran loose, dragging wooden sleds. Old men sat at tables in the shade of a bombed-out hotel, drinking slivovitz and playing chess. Beach chairs were everywhere. Entrepreneurs had set up makeshift stands, selling beer and soda, sunglasses and cigarettes. Families strolled about. A restaurant was open, music playing, sausages on the grill.

Chris and I had not brought our own ski gear, so we were forced to rent. The selection was poor—my skis, a decade-old pair of Elans, looked as though they'd been caught in the crossfire. "We used to have better equipment," said a woman named Lila, who was working at the rental shop, "but it was stolen by Serbs during the war." The rentals cost $7; a lift ticket, $9.

The line for the chair was long and disorganized. If one ever hoped to ski, this was no place for politeness. Even with my elbows out and my skis riding others' tails, I still spent half the wait moving backward. Dozens of NATO soldiers, in uniform but apparently enjoying a day off, were also skiing. I rode up with Chris. On the chair in front of us, a couple spent the entire ride tied in a kiss. Four runs were open, all groomed and fast, with a few places to sneak down the sides and make fresh tracks. (But not *too* far off the sides—though the area displayed a certificate from a French peacekeeping organization declaring the mountain free of land mines, I was still leery.)

Bosnians, for the most part, were strong, confident skiers. The hills may have been closed for half a decade, but nobody seemed rusty. There were only a handful of beginners, and even fewer snowboarders. Almost everyone owned their own equipment. I began the day, as did most skiers, by schussing the bottom half of the Olympic downhill course. The run, not surprisingly, transformed everyone into speed demons. I think we all had the same tape playing in our heads, of Johnson, hell-bent for glory, barreling crazy down the mountain. And so we each flew down the run, in deep tucks, launching off the rollers at red-line velocity, gunning for air time. Several people did this all day long, timing themselves on wristwatches or racing one another side by side, jeering and catcalling. One young skier skidded into the base area in a billow of snow-mist, looked up at an imaginary leaderboard, and raised his arms in fantasized victory. The few ski patrollers on the hill seemed not in the least concerned with interrupting the fun.

Off the T-bar, which was half the length of the chair, a slalom course was set up and racers, young and old, fast and not, lined up to participate. On an adjacent run, a couple of ski lessons were being taught, in inimitable ski-lesson style, the students standing along the sides of the slopes performing knee bends and pole plants. Several teenagers shouldered their skis and hiked above the lifts, kicking steps all the way to the summit. I watched as they descended in energetic fashion, cutting wide, sine-curve arcs into the heavy snow, scribbling tracks across the whole of Bjelasnica's bald spot. If there were land mines up there, they remained untriggered.

At lunchtime, on the restaurant's sundeck, I met up with Sinisa Kovac, a coach with the Bosnian national ski team who has skied at Bjelasnica since he was four years old—he seems to know every other person on the slopes. He had been working with some future prospects over at the slalom course. Three Bosnian racers, he told me, two men and a woman, are currently at World Cup level. Sinisa is 31 years old, a Croat; he sported long hair and mod sunglasses and a mysterious half grin that made everything he said take on a slight spin of sarcasm. In addition to coaching, he teaches biomechanics and physical education at the University of Sarajevo. During the siege, Sinisa was part of a special-forces unit with the Bosnian army. He carried three automatic weapons with him at all times.

We rode the lift together. The Bosnian Alps, low-slung and ridgy, spread out before us. There are plans, said Sinisa, for both a gondola and a hotel to be built here before the start of next ski season. At the top, we hiked uphill for a few minutes and Sinisa pointed out rocks he used to jump off when he was a kid, now unreachable by the lifts. When I asked about the war, he was hesitant to share his feelings. He said his family's house had burned down, and that several of his friends were now missing limbs, and that other friends had spent time in Serb-run concentration camps. "Life sucks, buy a helmet," he said, and then he skied off, full speed, legs wide apart like a racer's.

◆ ◆ ◆

After the lifts closed, I wandered over to the tables beneath the ruined hotel, and was roped into a game of chess and a glass of plum brandy by a man named Dinko, who lifted up his shirt to show me the entrance and exit wounds left by a bullet that had passed through his chest, somehow missing every vital organ. Even after I'd been checkmated twice, the area was still crowded. People seemed reluctant to leave.

It had been a beautiful day in the Sarajevo mountains, a mini-vacation, but even so, something was missing. Something intangible. I could see it in people's eyes. Rather than the typical ski-area feeling of unrestrained joy, there was more an acute sense of relief. There seemed to be the unspoken sentiment that this season of freedom may only be a respite. There was peace, but it was a tenuous one. Reminders of the fighting were everywhere. No matter where you placed your beach chair, it was impossible to miss the destroyed buildings, or the soldiers. There were no locals on the hill who didn't know at least 10 people who had perished in the fighting. Of Sarajevo's 300,000 citizens, nearly 12,000 were killed during the siege.

The horrors, though, weren't confined merely to town. Dr. Kulenović may consider the ski areas places of escape, but in truth they were scenes of some of the most egregious war crimes. Just down the road from Bjelasnica, at the base of a small ski hill called Igman, is the Olympic ski-jumping arena. One afternoon, Chris and I caught a cab there. A rope tow was running, and several people were skiing. It was at Igman, during the Sarajevo Games, that the great Finnish jumper Matti Nykaenen had won gold in the 90 meter jump, silver in the 70. Now, the ski jumps were cratered with blast holes. The start house atop each of them looked as though it were made of charcoal—a result of incendiary missiles. One area was cordoned off with thick yellow tape warning of land mines.

The podium where Nykaenen was awarded his medals was at the base of the jumping hill. Behind it stood a tall, triangular sculpture, made of cement. Before the war, the sculpture had been ornamented with the Olympic rings, the snowflake-shaped Sarajevo Olympic logo, and, encased in little plastic boxes, a soil sample from each of the 49 nations that sent athletes to the Winter Games—at the time, a record turnout. Two and one fifth of the Olympic rings remained attached. The other rings, and the logo, and most of the soil samples had been blown away. What was once a smooth cement wall was pocked top to bottom with bullet scars.

A NATO soldier stationed in the area, a German colonel named Jorgen Hillerkus, told me what had happened. "The ski hills were vital strategic positions," he said, speaking excellent English. "Whoever controlled the ski hills controlled access to Sarajevo, and so there was heavy fighting here. The Serbs held the hills for most of the war, and from here they'd send missiles into the city. When they captured Bosnian soldiers, they'd sometimes bring them up here and make them stand on this medal podium. Then they'd execute them."

I ran my hand over the jagged cement. The bodies had been buried; the blood washed away; the shell casings collected for sale back in town as souvenirs. Food was available at the base-lodge café. Magpies flitted and called. The skiers seemed to pay little attention to the charred ski jumps, or the ruined sculpture, or the armed soldiers. They seemed to be focusing on what was right. It was a sunny day, and the snow was soft. A lift was running. People were skiing.

♦ ♦ ♦

The morning after Chris and I visited Bjelasnica, we traveled to the ski hill on the Serb side. This required two taxis—one to take us to the edge of the Bosnian Federation, and another to drive us through the Serb Republic. Except in United Nations terms, Bosnia is two nations. There are different currencies, and different license plates. It is impossible to make a phone call from one side to the other.

As we rode through the Serb town of Pale—the athletes' village during the Games, and the Serb headquarters during the siege—Chris looked visibly nervous. He had been to Bosnia in wartime, and to have ventured into Pale during the fighting would have been seen as a suicide mission. The town, several blocks worth of tidy homes with red-tiled roofs, seemed hardly damaged; only a few outlying buildings were acned with small-arms fire. The mosques that were here before the war, though, were now gone.

The Serbian mountain, called Jahorina, was also in good condition. Jahorina, which opened in 1928, is Bosnia's oldest ski hill. All nine lifts that were in place for the Olympics were running, and several hotels were functioning normally, although we had to pass through a metal detector to gain admittance to the fanciest one. The rentals were top of the line. Only the summit lodge was destroyed. Several condominiums were gutted by fire, though I was told that the Serbs had torched these themselves—the homes were owned by Croat or Muslim families.

Otherwise, I was struck by the similarities between the two ski hills. And it wasn't merely the terrain, although Jahorina, too, is a gentle mountain, all the runs descending from a long, horseshoe-shaped ridge. It was again unseasonably warm, and it appeared as if the same crowd that had arrived in Bjelasnica yesterday had decided to follow Chris and me here, though likely not one person had. (Serbs, Croats, and Bosnian Muslims are all of the same racial origin, South Slavic, and visually they are indistinguishable from one another. Religion is the primary difference.)

At Jahorina's base area, the same music that I'd heard at Bjelasnica was playing—second-tier British and American pop—and the same food was being served: At every stand, the featured dish was *cevapčići*, spicy beef sausages tucked into spongy bread. The skiers were no better, and no worse. The reception I received at Jahorina was equally warm; the people seemed just as friendly. There was the same unmistakable presence of NATO troops. And, for me, there was the similar sense that some thread of joy was missing, overshadowed by relief, and pain, and worry.

As I skied, I thought about the possibility of the return of the Olympics. On the flight over, I had read *Bosnian Chronicle*, by Ivo Andrić, a Croat who had won the 1961 Nobel Prize in literature. One passage particularly struck me, and I'd circled it: "It seemed as if nothing in this country was immune to sudden, startling changes. Everything, at any moment, might become the opposite of what it seemed to be." If Andrić were right, then a second Olympics in Sarajevo was all but expected.

When Dr. Kulenović, in his office in downtown Sarajevo, had spoken to me about the bid for the Games his eyes had turned soft with tears. "The Olympics," he said, "are the only thing that can restore our city's image in the eyes of the world, and heal the wounds within." He said that the International Olympic Committee had allocated generous funds for repairs. Zerta Hall, walking distance from the center of town, the stadium where Katarina Witt had spun to gold, was struck by a missile during the first month of the war. It is now rebuilt.

When I'd toured Sarajevo's old city, which had avoided the brunt of the shelling, people crowded the streets, cell phones pressed to their ears, strolling past flower shops and cyber-cafés, a Benetton and a Burger King. The skyline was a pleasing commingling of the mosques' slender minarets and broad domes with the boxy steeples and gabled roofs of Orthodox and Catholic churches—a reminder of the time, not long ago, when Sarajevo was thought of as a place of religious liberalism, a city where nearly one-third of the marriages were interethnic. Why shouldn't such tolerance return?

I wanted to feel optimistic, but for some reason I could not. Over the past five centuries, Bosnia has been a place of seemingly constant conflict and rebellion. It was in Sarajevo, in 1914, that a young Serb named Gavrilo Princip assassinated Austrian Archduke Franz Ferdinand, igniting the first World War. During World War II, the ski hills had also been areas of intense fighting. The journalist David Rieff, in his book *Slaughterhouse: Bosnia and the Failure of the West*, writes that it is "the tragic, historic fate of Serbs, Croats, and Bosnian Muslims to try to kill each other off once every generation or so." In the most recent Bosnian war, there has been no real resolution. Several people in Sarajevo told me that if the NATO troops were to leave, fighting would restart the instant the last solider crossed the border.

There were hundreds of young Serbian men skiing on the hill. I watched some of them from the chairlift. I wondered which ones had sent missiles down upon Sarajevo, or had looted villages, or had tortured prisoners in concentration camps. I wondered how many were still itching to fight. This is not something I am accustomed to pondering at a ski area. The conclusion it led me to was a dark one. It is not the conclusion I wanted to make—it is not a forecast I hope is fulfilled—but I fear it is the more honest one: Another war is more likely in Sarajevo than another Olympics.

City Slider

I was walking up Park Avenue on my way to work, briefcase in hand, when the first snowflakes of winter finally fell. This was some time ago, during the brief period I lived in New York City and actually held somewhat of a real job, health insurance and all. It was late March—March 19, to be exact—and most New Yorkers were counting their blessings that the season had passed without a single snowfall. That is, until a storm cloud seemed to get hung up on the spire of the Empire State Building and began unloading its ballast of white stuff. Popcorn-size flakes cascaded down between the skyscrapers. Within twenty minutes Park Avenue was a mess of brown slush, honking taxis, miserable businesspeople, and one grinning pedestrian.

The grinner, of course, was me. As everyone on the street moaned and cursed and stampeded into the subways, I was mentally grappling with the details of a single, undeniable plan: *cross-country skiing in Central Park.* I had been waiting since the first cold day in October for an opportunity to slide through the nation's most famous urban playground, and I realized that this was probably going to be the year's only chance.

Reflexively, and utterly without permission from my boss (he was a kind man, with a rare appreciation of my passion for skiing), I raced back to my apartment, zigzagging through streets snarled with traffic, hurdling small puddles of chocolate-colored snowmelt, splashing the bottom third of my khakis with New York's permanently staining street-grime. Shirt, slacks, and briefcase were dumped on my bed. In record time, I changed into my ski clothes and hit the streets again, my right hand waving. A well-worn taxi dive-bombed the curb.

"Sixty-first and Broadway," I told the driver. I was in a slight frenzy; in bad weather, the long ride uptown could take the better part of an hour, and the radio was calling for the snow to taper off into rain at any moment. I needn't have worried. My cabbie was the type who simply invented new lanes when all the traditional ones were filled. He slalomed through the midtown traffic with Tomba-esque skill and skidded to a stop in front of Eastern Mountain Sports, the only place I knew of near the park that rented cross-country skis. The snow out-side the store was nearly ankle-high and getting higher, with no sign of a slowdown.

Skis, boots, and poles were $18 for the day. I gathered up my equipment, walked south for two blocks, and arrived at the Columbus Circle entrance to Central Park. The snow inside the park was just like the type that falls on mountains! It was white—bright white—and it lent the park an aura of tranquillity. Little piles had accumulated on the benches, like pillows, and the jagged rocks atop the stone walls that surround the park now appeared as smooth as icicles. Even the hillsides, usually splotchy and rock-strewn, looked like prime spots for a Flexible Flyer. I stepped into my gear and shoved off. Eight hundred and forty-three acres of undevel-oped Manhattan real estate awaited my tracks. After nearly six months of waiting, a few precious moments of solitude were just a couple of pole plants away.

Relative solitude, that is. Even though Central Park is celebrated as one of the most peaceful areas in Manhattan, the fact remains that it is still Manhattan. As I slid along the jogging path that rings the park, a steady stream of cars passed in the adjacent motorist lane. Their wheels kicked up small tsunamis of slush, and I had to weave back and forth on the path to avoid the brunt of the spray. In front of Umpire Rock, a boulder that's normally infested with manic preschoolers, two men sat forlornly on a bench, passing a paper bag back and forth. As I whisked by, one of them asked me for a quarter. Near Tavern on the Green, the park's well-known restaurant, I giant-slalomed through a maze of overloaded garbage cans. Passing one of the containers, I rammed my ski tip into something metallic. I reached down: Diet Coke can. Barren wilderness Central Park is not. I did, however, spot some wildlife. Approaching the park's Seventy-second Street entrance, I watched a rat the size of a sewing machine lumber across the path just in front of me. It left behind tiny pawprints, like inverted Braille dots, in the deepening snow.

I had not expected Central Park to offer the quintessential Nordic experience. Still, things were getting a mite depressing. Despite my maneuvering, more than a few of the wheel spurts had deposited themselves on my jacket. And around steam vents, where the snow was thin, my skis made terrible grinding noises as the bases rubbed against solid ground. My best chance for a worthwhile ski, I realized, was the Sheep Meadow.

The Sheep Meadow is a broad, gently sloped field encircled by a chain-link fence. It offers the smoothest, cleanest, grassiest area in Central Park. Even the Great Lawn, site of Simon and Garfunkel's famous concert, is too rocky and obstacle-laden (benches, backstops, boulders) to offer good skiing. So just beyond Tavern on the Green I waited for the light to turn red—not something one often does on a pair of skis—then shuffled across the slushy street and headed over to the Sheep Meadow.

Whereupon I encountered a problem. The gate to the meadow was closed and padlocked. A sign was attached to the fence:

SHEEP MEADOW CLOSED FOR SEASON

MEADOW OPENS FOR X-COUNTRY SKIING WHEN THERE IS 6"

SNOW COVER. USE OF CLOSED FIELD IS A VIOLATION OF PARKS

RULES AND REGULATIONS (SECTION 17) AND IS A MISDEMEANOR.

I couldn't believe it. I wait six months for this and now I have to wait for six inches? This was beyond preposterous— it may not *ever* snow six inches again in New York City.

I stuck my hand in the snow. It went in up to my wrist. From my fingertips to my wrist is a good five inches, at least. And it was still snowing hard. I looked around for a Parks Department official coming to unlock the gate. None. I looked around for a police officer coming to arrest scofflaws. None.

I took off my skis and hopped the damn fence.

The trees surrounding the meadow were glorious, branches thick with piled snow. The sounds of the city were muted. Only the slightest breath of wind worked its way across the field. The ground felt comfortable and spongy, and the snow here, free from grime, was perfectly powdery.

Even the New York skyscrapers, shadowy monoliths ascending from beyond the trees, looked peaceful through the steadily falling snow.

I made my own tracks. I romped among the trees, I sprinted across the flats, I slid placidly down the small hill. I circled the field five times, six times, seven. Beads of sweat formed on my forehead. The air tasted almost sweet, like a vanilla milkshake. The city disappeared behind a screen of swirling snow. For a few moments, I had full ownership of my own private slice of Manhattan.

But only for a few. Other fence-hopping skiers soon joined in, and we smiled at one another as we looped around the field. There were eight million New Yorkers out there and only a half dozen of us thought to play *with* the snow instead of against it. I never felt so city-savvy in my life.

Or so wet. By the time a group of teenagers jumped the fence and started a snowball fight, the spray that had drenched me earlier had worked its way to my skin. This was going to be complicated enough to explain to my boss without having to take a week off for sickness, so I decided to return home.

I waved adieu to my partners in crime—other urban dwellers with rural souls, who were probably playing hooky like me—climbed the fence once again, and hoisted my skis onto my shoulders. And as I was walking out of the park and back to the sporting goods store, past the slush puddles with crumpled pages of *The New York Times* floating in them like giant croutons, past taxi drivers who honked and cursed when I crossed at the DONT WALK sign, and past snowplows forming trenches of brownish gook on the sidewalks, the generous flakes of snow subtly shifted into rain.

A Saga of Iceland

" This has the potential to be a very large mistake," I told my friend and traveling companion, Hank de Vré. We were standing on the tarmac in front of the one-room airport in Isafjördhur, Iceland, a snowball's throw from the Arctic Circle. Encircling us were the Westfjords Mountains, which rose sharply from the dark waters of the Denmark Strait and brushed the clouds 2,000 feet later at summits sheared flat by glacial grinding.

The mistake was parked on the runway. It was, more or less, an airplane. If you were to take a port-a-potty, tip it on its side, paint it bright yellow, and attach a wooden propeller to the front and a pair of plastic wings to the top, you would have a fair representation of the plane in question. Hank, who is a professional photographer, thought the photo opportunities would be entirely grand if I got into the plane, landed on one of the flat-topped mountains, and skied down.

The skiing part I had no problem with. I was in Iceland, after all, to ski the type of runs that can only be found in Iceland. I had issues with the plane. Not the size, or the color, or even the less-than-aerodynamic shape—rather, I told Hank, it was the unnerving fact that *this guy built the whole thing in his basement.* I pointed at Örn Ingólfsson, our would-be pilot, who was whistling some Icelandic folk tune under his breath and tinkering with the propeller.

Örn was tall and sinewy, with eyes that can only be described as Icelandic blue: shockingly bright, like a sunny sky after you emerge from a dimly lit house. He had an aura about him of tightly wrapped intensity—he reminded me, somehow, of one of those wire-spring snakes stuffed into a can, ready to leap out at the slightest prodding. He was 40 but looked not a day over 30. Being a skier, I am normally attracted to such eccentrics, and I wanted to find some reason—any reason—to convince me that his airplane wasn't the lowest-priced nonstop to the hereafter. But then I noticed the plane's door. There, neatly stenciled in black letters, in English, was a single word: EXPERIMENTAL.

◆ ◆ ◆

Experimental, indeed. What better way to describe my ski trip to Iceland? Sure, if you want plain-Jane skiing, Iceland's got upward of two dozen small areas, with chairlifts and groomed runs and base lodges and all that. But that's not why I was hauling my gear all the way to Iceland. I was there because I'd heard that the place has 2,500-vertical-foot powder runs that will make hair stand on end in places you didn't even realize you had hair; because Iceland has more snow *right now* than Colorado has ever had; and, most of all, because the word "liability" isn't even in the Icelandic language. Which is how I ended up at the Isafjördhur airport with a pilot named Örn who was convinced he could land his mail-order airplane atop the biggest untracked bowl in all of Iceland.

When Hank and I had left New York, a few days earlier, we were on a regulation Icelandair jumbo jet, failing in our attempts to catch a bit of sleep on the overnight flight. We landed at Keflavík airport, 30 miles west of the capital city of Reykjavík. Here, in the southwest corner of Iceland, the glacial waters of the Atlantic break against a landscape the color and texture of dried oatmeal: mile after mile of lumpy volcanic rock, barren save for small tufts of gray-green grass. It is little surprise that NASA sent its astronauts to this area to train for their lunar missions.

Jóhann Jónsson, an official with the Iceland tourist board, picked us up at Keflavík and decided we required a dip in the Blue Lagoon, a few minutes drive from the airport. The lagoon was a curious place. From a distance it appeared as if the area were engulfed in smoke. From the shore, I felt as though I'd been cast into the heart of a giant machine—silver steam vents protruded from the lagoon's center, roaring like spring-melt waterfalls. The water bubbled ominously; steam clouded the air.

The water, we were assured, is perfectly safe. In fact, it's better than safe: The silica mud at the lagoon's bottom, when rubbed on your skin, is reputed to cure arthritis, muscle aches, and hangovers. And as for all the machinery, said Jóhann, it's simply a geothermal energy plant, tapping into Iceland's restless belly. Iceland, smaller than the state of Ohio, is a geological wonderland. Hot springs, volcanoes, lava flows, glaciers, and geysers (including Geysir, the geyser for which all geysers are named) abound, all of them churning and hissing and grinding away. Virtually all of Iceland's energy needs are fulfilled by harnessing hot water. There are even steam pipes running beneath the sidewalks of Reykjavík, keeping them free of snow year-round. In his novel *Journey to the Center of the Earth,* Jules Verne selected Mount Snaefell, in Iceland's uninhabited interior, as his portal to the planet's fiery innards.

So Hank and I hot-tubbed, Icelandic style, spreading white mud on our backs while the silver machines roared. Like most everything in Iceland these days, it was an odd, almost contradictory, combination of old and new. Ever since Iceland gained independence from Denmark, in 1944, the country has endeavored to shed hundreds of years of isolation at somewhat of a manic pace. American fast-food joints now abound. There is a Hard Rock Café. Heavy-metal music is king. A cell phone and a Web site and a hat with an NBA logo are considered de rigueur. In 1980, Vigdís Finnbogadóttir became the first woman to be elected president of a democratic country.

At the same time, though, Iceland retains a fierce grip on its past. By law, all citizens must have traditional Icelandic names; a list is provided by the government. Icelandic is the oldest living European language—1,000-year-old sagas read like yesterday's paper—and the country is so fearful of eroding its language that a government commission is responsible for creating medieval equivalents for words like "compact disc" and "fax machine." Artificial food coloring has recently been banned, depriving Icelanders of their favorite American food, M&Ms. (To make friends quickly, take a few bags with you. The 100 I brought were gone in three days.) The country has no army and virtually no crime. A stabbing is front page news, and prisoners are allowed to go home for the holidays.

As much as anything, it is Iceland's geographical seclusion—in the North Atlantic, between Greenland and Norway—that allows the nation to maintain a viable balance between past and present. Each Icelandic year sees 2,400 consecutive hours of darkness or dusk. In winter, traditional Iceland holds sway. It is a time for reading the ancient sagas (Iceland's literacy rate is 100 percent), for writing (as a percentage of population, Iceland has the largest number of published poets in the world), and for chess playing (per capita, the country leads the globe in grand masters). Then, just as strangely, come 100 days of almost continuous light, the sun bobbing about the horizon like a beachball adrift at sea. During summer, Western influences abound. Fashionable outfits are worn to go glacier skiing; the latest high-tech mountain bikes are pedaled into the interior. Hank and I visited in April, the ideal time for skiers—the sun is up 16 hours a day and the snow is at its deepest and softest.

April is also when Reykjavík awakens from its winter stupor. The capital, Iceland's first permanent settlement, was established by the Vikings in 874. As recently as 1800, only 300 people lived in town, 27 of whom were in jail for public drunkenness. Now, two thirds of Iceland's 250,000 people live in Reykjavík and its environs. Jóhann insisted we spend a night in the city before heading inland, promising us an Icelandic supper we would not soon forget.

We ate at Naust, a dark, subterranean restaurant with antique nautical paraphernalia hanging on the walls. Jóhann took charge, whispering conspiratorially to our waiter. Out came *brennivín,* 80-proof firewater known throughout Iceland as the "black death." One shot. Two. Three. We were ready, Jóhann declared, for *hákarl,* a local delicacy that proves why Icelanders are such rugged people. Hákarl, as I later found out, is putrefied shark meat. It has been buried in a gravel pit for six months to ensure proper decomposition. Even birds that normally eat carrion won't touch this stuff, so it can be buried anywhere. It looks like small chunks of tuna. It smells like ammonia. I took a mouse-nibble and I had to shut my eyes and push my hands against my temples in order to stifle the urge to vomit. Hákarl is the worst-tasting food I have ever sampled. It is so bad I don't think anything else I've tried can qualify as second worst. The Texas Department of Corrections, I feel, should investigate hákarl's potential for punitive uses.

A large glass of brennivín prepared us for round two. Out came *blódmör:* sheep's blood packed in suet. Then *lifrapylsa:* sheep's liver pudding. And then *hrútspungur:* pickled rams' testicles. Not all the food in Iceland is straight from an Indiana Jones movie. We also ate herring—pickled, curried, cherried, you name it—as well as halibut, Icelandic lamb (especially delicious), reindeer, and puffin. In the end, however, it was the prices that nearly killed us. Food in Iceland is ridiculously expensive, and our gustatory adventure at Naust was no exception. The bill for the three of us was $500.

◆ ◆ ◆

Come morning, Hank and I learned why brennivín is called the black death. Gale-force storms raged in our heads, while on our tongues sat the not-so-faint aftertaste of hákarl. In the midst of our blackness, however, emerged Ingi and Oskar, a pair of guides from Add Ice, a Reykjavík-based adventure outfitter. Icelandic people, I must say, are extraordinarily beautiful. This includes both women and men. I am not alone in this opinion—an absurdly disproportionate number of Icelanders have won the Ms. Universe or Mr. Universe titles. I very nearly had to be treated for whiplash after sitting on a park bench in Reykjavík and attempting to surreptitiously watch women stroll by. Ingi and Oskar, meanwhile, were of Chippendale's ilk. They looked, and even spoke, somewhat like Hans and Franz, the bodybuilders from the old *Saturday Night Live* skit. They arrived with their four-wheel-drive Toyota HiLux, which was named *Utlaggin*— Outlaw. It was time to go glacier-skiing.

We drove east, along the southern coast of Iceland. To our right was the Atlantic, pounding relentlessly against a jagged coastline. To our left, 200-foot cliffs rose from grassy plains. Scores of puffins sat nesting along the shore; Icelandic horses, with their long golden manes trailing behind them like halos, galloped in the fields. Here and there, at a break in the cliffs, a waterfall surged forth, returning glacial water to the sea. Even the weather was glorious, a breezy 40 degrees. Despite Iceland's name—a nightmare for a ski-area marketing director if ever there was one—the temperatures are not particularly icy, averaging 34 degrees in winter, 50 in summer. The only thing missing, it seemed, were trees.

"What do you call two trees in Iceland?" asked Ingi, in flawless English, setting up a typically self-deprecating Icelandic joke.

"A forest," chimed in Oskar.

"What's three trees?"

"A jungle."

Iceland's glaciers, which cover 11 percent of the nation's land mass, seem strangely situated. They're simply *there*—they appear to rise from the Icelandic plain with no geographical warning. From high in the air, I imagine, Iceland resembles an assortment of vanilla cakes sitting on a round kitchen table. Ingi and Oskar took us to *Eyjafjallajökull*—the Mountains of the Island Glacier. The glacier began, quite literally, in a farmer's backyard. Ingi swerved the Utlaggin off the paved road, around a barn, through a herd of sheep, and up onto the snow.

When the slope of the glacier grew steep, Ingi stopped and let most of the air out of the tires, so that the Utlaggin could float atop the snow. Two hours later, more than seven miles into the glacier, we arrived at our cabin. Or at least at what Ingi and Oskar assured us was a cabin. It looked more like a large mound of ice. We grabbed axes and pounded away. After an hour, a door was discovered. Soon we were actually able to open it. Inside were four bunks and a kitchenette. Outside, for 360 degrees flush to the horizon, the world was white: mountains of snow, valleys of snow, large plains of wind-sculpted snow. Nowhere was there even the faintest sign of another living thing. We were home.

The Outlaw doubled as our ski lift. We clicked into our gear and grabbed a rope connected to the rear bumper. Ingi jammed the gas, and Hank and Oskar and I were off like a shot, our skis rattling across the glacial expanse. At the foot of a modest glacial peak, we put our boards on our backs and crampons on our boots, and slogged to the summit.

The skiing was difficult. Beneath two or three inches of granular was a rather large base of ice—2,500 feet, according to Ingi. And whenever we skied over a thin crack—something that's unavoidable on a glacier, and signals that a buried crevasse may be lurking below—my heart bobbled for a tick as the snow sank beneath my skis, often settling three or four inches.

But we carved tracks, dozens of them, slapping our S's on as many of the glacial hills as we could climb. We sailed off finely carved lips, schussed into long, flat valleys, and listened to the flutelike sounds of the wind curling into dozens of yawning crevasses. On the truck-tows back up, I leaned back and carved water-ski-style turns, drinking mouthfuls of pure Icelandic air. It was past 10 P.M. when the skies finally began to darken. Ingi and Oskar dug a hole in the ice, threw in some charcoal, and roasted a leg of Icelandic lamb. The four of us sat in front of our half-buried cabin, enthralled, as the setting sun turned 200 square miles of ice and snow the color of a ripe strawberry.

♦ ♦ ♦

The next evening, Hank and I caught an Icelandair flight from Reykjavík to Isafjördhur, the largest town in the Westfjords. The Westfjords is Iceland's claw-shaped northwest region, reaching out to pinch Greenland. It is also, according to Ingi and Oskar, the best spot in the nation to find long, difficult ski descents.

There was no shortage of snow. The sides of Isafjördhur's roads were lined with piles 20 feet high. There was also no shortage of mountains—flat-topped, rock-ribbed, and scary steep. Most of them, I soon learned, had never been skied. The villages, cluttered with colorful corrugated-steel homes (wood is a rarity in Iceland), are scattered at the bases of these peaks, along the banks of a hundred or more fjords.

The town of Isafjördhur extends into one of these narrow inlets, on a sand spit the shape of a curled fist. Like the rest of Iceland, Isafjördhur is spotless, a result of the national government's policy of hiring all out-of-work teenagers to clean the harbors and streets. Rusty fishing boats bob up and down in the dark-green water, which surrounds the town on three sides, reflecting the mountains. Isafjördhur has two restaurants, one hotel, and no T-shirt shops by my way of thinking, a perfect skier's town.

Perfect, that is, except for one thing: Besides some T-bars strung up a few slopes, the mountains are accessible only by nontraditional means. This is how Örn Ingólfsson, the mad pilot of Isafjördhur, entered my life. Word had passed through town that a pair of foreign skiers had arrived, and Örn made his way to the hotel. We met in the dining room. Örn told us that it would take hours, or perhaps days, to climb even one of Isafjördhur's mountains, and to do so we'd need ropes and skins and other gear we hadn't brought with us and wasn't available in town. We'd be far happier, he said, if we flew up in his two-seater, which was equipped with special snow-landing gear. He'd show us his machine the next morning, he said. Our conversation bordered on the surreal.

"Where did you buy your plane?" I asked.

"I sent away for it. It cost 11,000 American dollars, not including an engine."

"What about the engine?"

"I took it out of my snowmobile."

"Have you had the thing inspected?"

"Yes, I inspected it myself."

"Is it safe to land on snow?"

"Yes, and if we tumble, at least the snow is soft."

"Have you taken up skiers before?"

"Yes, one time I did."

"Are you an experienced pilot?"

"Yes. Are you an experienced skier?"

"Yes."

We shook. No contracts to sign, no mention of price.

The next morning rose cloudless and shining, an Icelandic rarity. We warmed up on the local hill, Selja-landsdal, sharing the slopes with dozens of young racers, most skiing extremely fast and profoundly straight, partici-pants in a countrywide race program that is Iceland's version of Little League. Skiing is Iceland's second most popular sport, behind soccer, and each Icelandic school offers an official day off so that students can go skiing.

The ski area was small and the mountains beckoned, so we hitched over to the airport. There, for the first time, I saw the plane. I peered inside. On the dash were four meters—air speed, water temperature, altitude, and RPM. There was also a snowmobile engine's starter cord, and a clear plastic tank in which the level of fuel could easily be seen. "That way," explained Örn, "we don't need a fuel gauge." A small sticker was pasted over a spot where I thought the radio should be: PASSENGER WARNING—THIS AIRCRAFT IS AMATEUR BUILT AND DOES NOT COMPLY WITH THE FEDERAL SAFETY REGULATIONS FOR STANDARD AIRCRAFT.

"I don't know," I told Hank, who was practically drooling about the photo prospects. His eyebrows arched like a pleading child's. "There's 2,000 feet of powder out there," he said, grabbing my arm. "And no one has ever skied it before. *Ever.*" In his sunglasses I could see the shining reflection of a massive field of snow. A steep untracked soft sunny massive field of snow. I climbed into the copilot seat.

Örn yanked the starter cord and the airplane sputtered to life. We plodded down the runway, 400 pounds of plane rumbling like a bed equipped with Magic Fingers, and slipped subtly off the tarmac. Wind rushed through the open doors. The red and blue and gray roofs of Isafjördhur's homes shrank away fast, and the sharp-faced slopes of the mountains filled the horizon. We reached top speed, 60 miles per hour, and the little plane buzzed contentedly as we spiraled upward. The cockpit was so small that Örn and I sat shoulder to shoulder, and I could feel the muscles in his arm tensing every time he nudged the control stick.

After several minutes of ascending, Örn banked around the largest of the plateau-topped mountains and readied for a landing. The wind was stronger than expected, and the snow slicker, and as the plane's runners touched the snow, we began to skid. The plane seemed on the verge of flipping over—that same feeling you get when you lean too far back in a chair and are about to tip—till Örn cut the engine and saved the landing. I got out of the plane and gave the ground a full-on Pope kiss.

Örn took off again, to bring Hank up so he could shoot pictures from the air, and I was alone. The silence was absolute. There wasn't a bird or a bush or a single pawprint. Even the wind was gone. The mountain's top was smooth as a frozen lake, half a mile long, a quarter mile wide. From where I stood, I could see a hundred more mountains, each with dozens of powder chutes, each with open bowls, each waiting for Örn's passengers to lay down first tracks. With a few helicopters, a savvy marketer, and some luck, I thought, this would be an unparalleled heli-ski destination. With even more luck, I realized, it will never become a heli-ski destination.

The buzz of Örn's approaching airplane was my signal, and I launched into the snowfield in front of me. The bowl was steep, at least 40 degrees, and the backs of my skis skidded a bit on the first few turns. But I soon found my rhythm and the slope opened up in front of me, smooth and forgiving, and I let my speed go unchecked. The snow was exquisite corn, the chunky kind that pops up into your mouth. I reeled off 100 turns, neat and round, then 100 more, before my thighs were on maximum burn and the slope started to level out. Still, I puffed out another 30 before pulling up beside a deserted road. It was one of the finest runs of my life.

And then it got better. First one van pulled up, then two, and the next thing I knew I was being interviewed by both Icelandic television stations. News of my collaboration with Örn had gotten around, and the cameramen had managed to film most of my run from the roof of the airport. Off-piste skiing in the Westfjords is an uncommon event. The reporters wanted to talk with the foreigner who was so interested in skiing where the lifts don't go.

That evening, after the first of five days in which Hank and I would ski dozens of Westfjords mountains—for which Örn, who moonlights as an electrician, refused any payment other than gas money—I rushed up to my hotel room to watch the 10 o'clock news. While a commentator babbled away in Icelandic, I saw my run and relived every turn.

It was just about time for the Icelandic sunset, and already long shadows had formed in the mountains. I opened my window, to drink in more of the Icelandic air, and I heard a faint, familiar buzz. Up above the mountains, where the sun still shone, was Örn, alone in his plane, barrel-rolling through the wispy clouds.

Leap of Faith

It dawned on me, soon after my coach asked if I was ready for my first ski jump, that you can never be ready for your first ski jump. You can learn about technique until you're a walking instruction book; you can be as agile as a world-class gymnast; you can meditate until you're ready for monkhood. But when it comes time to actually speed down the ramp and launch yourself into flight, you are entering a realm that has to be experienced before it can be understood. You have to make a literal leap of faith.

My coach, Chris Hastings, understood this dilemma. But Chris didn't have time to wait. It was a cold February day at the Olympic Jumping Complex in Lake Placid, New York, and Chris was heading out of town in a few hours to attend a meet. If I didn't want to jump, he said, it would be perfectly understandable. But if I did, the time was now. An Olympic ski-jump arena is no place for common sense to prevail, I figured, so I grabbed my gear and headed for the jump.

Why? That, of course, is the question that pervades a ski jumper's life. Why do people devote years to learning how to fly 400 feet off an oversized, snow-covered ramp? It was my first question, in fact, as I made some preliminary inquiries several winters ago into one of the few ski-related activities I knew nothing about. Jumpers, at least American ones, certainly don't do it for the glory. The U.S. hasn't won an Olympic medal since Anders Haugen took the bronze in 1924. They don't do it for money. The Lake Placid team, from which most Olympians emerge, is so poorly funded it can't even afford its own van. The main reason they jump, it turns out, is a primal one: They do it for effect.

"Effect" is what ski jumpers call the lift they feel as they sail off the end of the ramp and into the sky. It is a sensation that induces such euphoria, Chris told me during our initial phone conversation, that it makes everything you have ever done before pale in comparison. This piqued my interest.

"Everything?" I asked.

"Everything," he repeated.

"*Everything?*"

"*Everything.*"

I was tantalized. Then Chris said that if I came up to the jumping complex for a weekend of training, he'd teach me enough to let me experience it myself. I called his bluff, and booked a flight.

The Lake Placid complex, nestled amid the evergreen-covered Adirondacks, has four jumps. The two big ones, a 90-meter and a 70-meter, were used in the 1980 Winter Games. They are made of concrete and steel, and loom solidly above the landscape like a pair of modernist Mayan temples. I found them scary to even look at. Off to one side, tucked in the trees, is a more friendly seeming 40-meter ramp, made of wood. Beyond that is a small 15-meter training jump, which looks like an oversized playground slide.

The locker room is located beneath the 90-meter jump, behind a brown door with large yellow lettering that reads JUMPERS ONLY. Inside, a gaggle of teenaged boys—ski jumping, at the top levels, is almost an exclusively male pursuit—were tumbling on mats, leaping over pommel horses, and performing pull-ups on ceiling pipes. A chocolate Lab named Jake was doing his own exercises. It was here that I first met Chris Hastings. Chris competed in the 1988 Calgary Olympics, and then turned to coaching. Ski jumping is not for the aged: Chris retired from competition at 23. When I met him, he was 29; all of his students were under 20.

Chris and I walked out to the 70-meter jump to watch practice—it takes about two years of training to work your way up to the 70, and another two or so before you're ready for the 90. A 13-year-old named Taylor Hoffman, one of America's top prospects, descended the inrun, accelerating in a matter of seconds to highway speeds, cutting through the air with an audible sizzle. He separated from terra firma. Then, as placidly as a conductor taking a bow, Taylor leaned out over his ski tips and floated for several seconds, his body motionless save for the subtlest of balance adjustments—a flick of the wrist, a flex of the ankle—before touching down, one foot in front of the other, on the landing hill. Though it seems otherwise on television, jumpers are never more than 20 feet off the ground, as their flight follows the curve of the landing hill. Ski jumping is no more dangerous, in terms of injury rate, than alpine skiing.

When done correctly, ski jumping appears more like a modernist dance—a kind of extended jeté—than an athletic event. The judging reflects this: Style points are an essential part of a competitor's score. "An adolescent's body, and mentality, is perfect for jumping," said Chris, explaining why I was nearly three times the age of the average rookie. "The lighter and more fearless you are, the better."

We went back to the locker room, and Chris presented me with my jumping equipment. My skis looked like pontoons: 235 centimeters long, twice as wide as alpine skis, with no edges and only the slightest of curves at the tips. Mounted atop them were telemark-style cable bindings that allowed my heels to lift freely. My boots looked and felt like basketball shoes, only with higher, stiffer backs. My one-piece jumping suit was made of a neoprene-like material called elasthan. It was blindingly pink; had I been given a choice of color, this would not have been my first one. The whole ensemble was topped off with a heavily scratched helmet.

My first assignment was to familiarize myself with the gear. It's essential, said Chris, that I learn how to stop. This wasn't something I had expected to be difficult—it was the go part I was worried about. It turns out, though, that maneuvering to stop on a pair of jumping skis, which are designed for stability rather than turning, feels like carving a turn in a foot of mud (something I've actually done—long story, not worth it). With the free-heel bindings, soft boots, and absence of poles, even gliding down the gentlest of hills required all my powers of coordination.

I learned the proper inrun tuck—skis apart, weight forward, arms trailing along my sides—by schussing down the landing slope of the 70-meter jump. My skis were so unwieldy I felt as though I were standing on a pair of runaway tobog-gans. This was not a comforting feeling. As I reached top speed, I found myself almost cataleptic with fear. And I hadn't even left the ground.

Later, still on the ground, I learned how to land—one foot thrown forward to improve balance, knees bent to absorb impact. I practiced by making a few insignificant leaps off the 15-meter hill, which is so small it doesn't really count as a ski jump. Chris and I discussed at length a jumper's tech-nique in the air: To achieve an airfoil position that will give you maximum glide, your head should be so far forward you can practically lick the tips of your skis. Chris was pleased with my progress. He scheduled me for a jump off the 40-meter the next morning.

Moving from the 15 to the 40 is like going from a nursery slope to a double diamond. (The 70 and 90 are strictly in the realm of the extreme.) I didn't feel quite prepared to make this transition, but my desire to feel the effect outweighed my fears. So I signed a waiver, one peppered with cheery words like "paralysis" and "dismemberment" and "death," then ascended the 259 wooden steps, skis over my shoulder, to reach the start platform. I placed my skis on the starting line, tips sticking out over the inrun, and strapped my boots into place. I adjusted my helmet, put on my gloves, and lowered my goggles. I crouched into my inrun position and waited for Chris's start signal.

Ski jumping is an all-or-nothing proposition. There is no such thing as half a ski jump; anything less than full effort is the surest way to get injured. Yet at the same time, it's not a stunt like bungee jumping, where the only challenge is stepping off the edge. During a ski jump there is so much to remember in so short a time—form in the inrun, position in the air, technique during landing—that it is best not to recall anything at all.

"A jumper doesn't think when he jumps," Chris had said before sending me up the steps. "He just reacts."

"But when do I start getting out of my inrun crouch?" I asked him. "When do I get ready to land?"

"When it feels right," he told me. "Don't worry, you'll know."

Needless to say, I worried. From the top of a ski jump, the landing area cannot be seen; the hill merely curves beneath your field of vision. There is no final destination to focus on. This is most disconcerting. For all you know, you are leaping into a bottomless abyss. By the time Chris waved his arms to signal that the jump was ready, the inside of my gloves were slick with sweat. The opening images of *ABC's Wide World of Sports* played like an endless loop in my head. I took several breaths, attempting to quell the thumping in my chest. It was in vain. I thought about the shame of quitting, the idiocy of jumping, and the agony of defeat. Finally, I thought about effect.

I allowed my skis to slide onto the inrun. As I accelerated to 40 miles per hour, I watched my ski tips flutter and struggled to keep them parallel. The wind roared in my ears, my vision tunneled—the trees along the sides blurred to walls of solid green—and I realized, in a fleeting thought, how absurdly fast I was going. There was nothing I could do to slow down. I raced toward the evergreen sprigs placed as a visual reference across the end of the ramp, and then, soon enough, right over them and off the edge.

The sudden weightlessness was startling. I felt oddly detached from my senses. It was as if the laws of physics had been declared unconstitutional, and I was now floating upward in a giant soap bubble. Everything was silent, a ringing silence, like the kind you hear after walking out of a loud concert. My eyes shot wide open, unblinking—at least in my mind's replay I don't recall blinking. As Chris had promised, there was no formal thinking going on while I was in the air. I could see, and I could react, but in the deeper regions of the cerebral cortex, everything was idling on maintenance mode. I recall sucking in a large gulp of air, and at the same time feeling a delicate tingling sensation, as if I had just stepped into a hot tub. This was accompanied by an exquisite moment of invincibility—I felt almost *safe*—in which I was abruptly aware that everything about me was blissfully, perfectly, ethereally serene. Without question, I had experienced an instant of effect.

The sensation passed almost immediately, though, and the ground rushed up to meet me, about 70 feet from my takeoff point. I landed clumsily and threw myself into a skidding stop. My legs began trembling and I had to sit down, right there on the snow. Chris ran over to congratulate me, but I was almost too deep in shock to respond. A patina of giddiness came over me. And at that moment, I realized, what I wanted more than anything else in the world was to rush back up the steps and do it all again.

A few minutes later, that's exactly what I did.

Vision at Yellowknife

The first flash of green across the nighttime sky was so startling that I lost my balance. My ski tips crossed and I went down hard on the snow-covered ice of the Great Slave Lake. My headlamp flew off, skittered across the smooth surface like a hockey puck, and went out. It was pitch dark, but only for a moment. A second flash, bright as a lightning bolt, leapt from the eastern horizon and sailed above me in a boomerang-shaped arc, pulsating, shimmering, and finally dividing into a school of neon-green waves. Goose bumps prickled across my skin and I lay there on the ice, too entranced to move. I had traveled to the very edge of civilization to witness the aurora borealis, and it was about to burst into full bloom.

The Northwest Territories, where I had gone to see the lights, is a vast Canadian region that extends from Baffin and Ellesmere Islands, just west of Greenland, to the Yukon Territory, which abuts Alaska. It is more than a third the size of the United States, yet home to only 55,000 people, one fourth of whom live in the city of Yellowknife. One local described his homeland to me this way: "It is so flat here that you can watch your dog run away for two days." He was incorrect only in that dogs do not run away in Yellowknife. There is nowhere to run to. The nearest major city, Edmonton, is a 22-hour drive south. A polar desert, frozen and wind-scoured and virtually uninhabited, encircles Yellowknife for hundreds of miles in every direction. This desert is known, quite aptly, as the Barrenlands.

The Barrenlands are possibly the finest area in North America from which to glimpse the aurora borealis. The aurora, also known as the northern lights, is a natural phenomenon that had been described to be me by otherwise nonreligious friends as "transcendent" and "spiritual" and "otherworldly." Even in the retelling, my friends' faces would assume appearances of radiant disbelief. Nobody, though, could quite specify what the lights actually looked like. And so I decided to travel to the far north myself, during the dark of winter, when the chance of an auroral display is at its highest.

I arrived at the Yellowknife airport via Calgary, in an airplane that was half filled with passengers and half filled with cargo. My first stop, after securing a room at the Hotel Yellowknife, was in Overlander Sports, in downtown Yellowknife, to rent a pair of cross-country skis. What better way to see the aurora, I figured, than to escape the city lights by skiing into the Barrenlands.

A salesperson at Overlander gave me the phone numbers for Jean Bristow-McCann, president of the Northwest Territories Ski Division, and Jonny Graves, who has resided in Yellowknife for 20 years. Both women are members of the Yellowknife Ski Club, a town-run cross-country center. They agreed at a moment's notice to give me a tour, and picked me up at my hotel. Both Jean and Jonny are tall and lean, with freely flowing laughs and an absolute imperviousness to the biting cold. They each bore the healthy, outdoorsy glow and stylish lack of style that is often referred to as "granola," yet at the same time there was an air about them of tough-as-nails intensity. I was sure they were equally comfortable on cross-country skis as they were handling a shotgun, or an axe, or the throttle of a snowmobile.

From the base shack of the Yellowknife Ski Club, Jean and Jonny lead me north, along the shoreline of the Great Slave Lake, where Yellowknife is situated. The Great Slave (named after the Slavey Indians) remains frozen more than half the year and offers the area's most consistent skiing surface—despite Yellowknife's location, 150 miles from the Arctic Circle, it receives less than three feet of snow each winter.

We skied first near New Town, where the sterile government buildings are located—arctic architecture, with few exceptions, is a case of function (e.g., How do we keep this place warm?) wholly eclipsing form. Yellowknife is the capital of the Northwest Territories and one of the world's major gold-mining towns. It is home to an odd amalgam of people: government workers, rough-hewn miners, and Inuit and Indian hunters and fishermen. Sixteen percent of Yellowknife's population is composed of native peoples, and the town has *eight* official languages: Chipewyan, Cree, Dogrib, English, French, Gwich'in, Inukitut, and Slavey. The signs on the government buildings are written in so many languages, some of which look like chemistry equations, that a visitor is likely to feel as if a United Nations conference is in town.

A quarter mile beyond New Town we passed beside Old Town, a haphazard collection of mobile homes and plywood cabins inhabited primarily by gold miners. Colorful, tattered flags flapped from rooftop poles; the cabins' outer walls were covered with old street signs, expired license plates, rusty automobile parts, and other materials most likely hauled from the junkyard. Old Town had both a celebratory and a somber feel to it, as if a Mardi Gras party had been held there several years ago, but no one had bothered to take the decorations down.

Late in the afternoon, my guides swung back and headed for home. I continued north, alone, traveling over the snow-swept ice until it seemed as if I were the last person left on

Earth. The crusty snow cracked like stale bread beneath my skis. There were no defining landmarks, only wind-sculpted snow and cotton-ball clouds. There was hardly any color. Even the sun, low in the sky, appeared milky white. The only signs of life were a few piles of caribou scat, and meandering sets of hoofprints.

I skied away from town in an unbending line. The landscape before me was a blank sheet extending to a featureless horizon. My eyes, with nothing to focus on, were unable to accurately register distances. I could not decide if something on the snow was a large object far away or a small object fairly close. This visual phenomenon is due to both the pureness of the arctic air, which prevents distant features from appearing fuzzy because there is little particulate matter in the atmosphere, and to the barren landscape, which *has* no distant features. It can play bizarre tricks with your vision. In severe cases, called Fata Morganas, the mind can concoct detailed mirages—early explorers, when mapping the territories, charted mountain ranges and islands that did not exist. I experienced my own mirage when I became entranced by a dark, steaming volcano that came into view on the horizon. Only when I skied closer did I realize that I had been staring at a cone-shaped mound of fresh caribou dung.

The sun disappeared quickly. I had been out for several hours already, and as the sky faded from navy blue to black, I turned around and began following my tracks back to

Yellowknife. Before I was halfway home, the first streak of the aurora ignited the heavens and I found myself sprawled on my back, headlamp several feet away, watching a show so dazzling I scarcely moved for almost two hours.

The display began with a few quick flashes of green, separated by long moments of darkness. Slowly the streaks merged, like drops of mercury gathering together, and there appeared a single wall of lambent green light, hanging from the heavens and undulating like a curtain in front of an open window.

I can tell you that the aurora occurs in the polar regions of the planet, where charged ions streaming away from the sun interact with the Earth's magnetic field, and that the energy created from this interaction is released as visible light. I can tell you that the lights hover between 60 and 250 miles above the earth, and can move at 700 miles per hour. But this feels as satisfying as explaining that a Mozart concerto is a sound made by a collection of musical instruments. I can also tell you the Inuit explanation, which says that the lights are torches held up by the gods to provide aid for wintertime hunting. They say that you can communicate with the lights by whistling softly.

So of course I whistled. The curtain of green light wavered for a few minutes, as though straining to hear me. It pulsated, floating from one horizon to the next. The movements were gentle, as if the aurora were made of tissue paper and any undue pressure would tear it apart. Abruptly, though, there was a dramatic rise in activity, and the waves of green morphed into strange crimson spikes, which hammered downward in violent bursts, diving so close to the Earth I felt I could reach out and touch one. These movements, too, eventually slowed, and soon the sky above me was filled with a kaleidoscopic montage of pastel colors and amorphous shapes, all moving at different speeds, threaded through with what looked like wisps of gray smoke. As the lights danced, I soared with them, encountering the same feelings of vertigo one does in a vivid dream about flying. Something I had known my whole life, the night sky, was suddenly alien. I felt exhilarated and unsettled and overwhelmed, all at once.

I lay on the ground until my entire body was numb with cold. In the arctic regions, hypothermia is a constant danger. So I forced myself up, clicked into my skis, and recovered my headlamp. The bulb was broken. For an instant, I panicked, then I remembered: The deities' torches were still blazing away. I glided back to Yellowknife with ease, navigating by the ever-changing glow.

The Mad River Cult

I ripped my ski pants wide open—ripped 'em from one knee right up the inseam and straight down to the other knee. I had been slaloming through a tight stand of trees at Mad River Glen, Vermont, when abruptly, my line ended. Swiftly approaching a full-grown pine and a human-size birch sapling, with no room between them, I chose the sapling and cruised into it at high speed. I flipped forward, clutching the trunk, then somersaulted off like a pole-vaulter, to the accompaniment of a prolonged rip, and divoted the snow with my forehead. Things like that can happen at Mad River.

My three partners—Mad River tree ninjas all—had seen me crash. Fingers were pointed at my legs; there was much sniggering. I looked down. Strips of nylon dangled from my pants like Tibetan prayer flags.

The pants were too tattered for slopeside duct-taping, but given the snow conditions—a rare mother lode of deep, talcy East Coast powder—stopping for the day was out of the question. Stopping for five minutes was out of the question. So I skied all afternoon in a pair of pants my mother would call a *shmatte*, which is Yiddish for, among other things, an article of clothing unfit for a scarecrow. Nobody at the ski area gave me so much as a second glance. At Mad River, people tear their pants open all the time.

◆ ◆ ◆

It's possible you don't know anything about Mad River Glen. The place is small, after all, with only a 2,000-vertical-foot drop and just one lift to the summit. This lift is a single chair—as in one person at a time—and is powered by an engine that sounds like a sack of potatoes being run through a clothes dryer. Mad River's owner, Betsy Pratt, wouldn't dream of replacing it. She views grooming, snowmaking, trail-widening, or anything that even smacks of modernization as downright heretical. Something new at Mad River means it's been added since the invention of the plastic ski boot. And there isn't much new. The on-mountain communication system is via World War II–era field phones. The base-lodge cash register needs to be cranked to ring up a sale.

The locals' devotion to the area borders on the absurd. Mad River is one of the last bastions of truly challenging, play-it-as-nature-drops-it, lawsuits-be-damned skiing in North America. When there's ice at the area, which is often, the locals not only ski ice, they genuinely seem to enjoy skiing ice. When there are exposed rocks, which is always, they not only leave P-tex behind, they apparently *like* leaving P-tex behind. When the bumps are bulletproof, they ski bullet-proof bumps. They ski Mad River when the base consists solely of a solid glaze. No complaints; no desire to ski any-where else.

The funny thing is, they could easily ski anywhere else. For all its separatist leanings, Mad River, located in the Green Mountains of central Vermont, is surrounded by high-tech superpowers like Killington, Stowe, Okemo, and Sugarbush. Yet only Mad River, a fraction the size of its neighbors, with no resort facilities, has a cult following. That's because only Mad River has seen the intermediate-pandering, golf-course-adding, five-course-lunching, featureless-grooming ways of the modern ski industry and decided to flip it the bird.

To a small but passionate group of skiers, such bravado has inspired reverence. Mad River's red-and-white bumper stickers, free to all visitors, have become the pirate flags of the ski community. It's a worldwide phenomenon—I've seen them on cars in Jackson Hole, in a barroom in Montana, on a lift shack in North Dakota, on the side of a tram in Val d'Isère. Their eight-word message, printed in simple block letters, is the hard-core skier's haiku: MAD RIVER GLEN—SKI IT IF YOU CAN.

◆ ◆ ◆

For five wild days a few Januarys ago, I tried to become one of the skiers who has. I rented a room at the Mad River Barn, a red-paneled 19th-century farm building now serving as a guest house. The Barn, owned by Betsy Pratt, is the only lodging within two miles of the mountain. Waitsfield, the closest town, is six miles away. The Mad River Valley is refreshingly undeveloped. There are HORSE XING signs, and cow pastures, and covered bridges, but not a single traffic light. The Barn is run with the same relaxed attitude as the ski hill. If I had a case of the midnight munchies, I could wander into the kitchen and fix myself a snack; when I wanted a beer, I could pour myself a brew and leave two bucks on the bar. I never did get a key to my room (I'm not even sure there are room keys), and all week I simply left my door unlocked.

The Barn, I was told, is Mad River's hot spot. This proved one thing: There ain't much nightlife at Mad River. I arrived on a Saturday evening—Patrolman's Platter night—when the Barn's weekly leftovers are served to dirt-poor locals for dirt cheap. About a dozen Mad River regulars, all men, showed up. They had the squint-eyed stare, permanent hat-head, and mellower-than-mellow demeanor of people who've spent entirely too much of their lives on a pair of skis. I liked them immediately. Also, they had beards. There was more facial hair in that room than anyplace I'd ever been, whiskers hanging off jaws like strands of spaghetti. It's been said you can't join the Mad River ski patrol if you've shaved in the past 10 years, and I believe it.

We talked skiing. Tele John told me to ski with my pockets inside out, to prevent them from filling with snow. Casey the Fisherman said everything he remembered from school he learned on the single chair—that's where he did his homework. Eric the Deadhead outlined plans for a cliff jump on tele skis and said I could call him Tedder, short for telemark shredder. Kyle the Stockbroker mentioned his Harvard education, Wall Street wealth, and fantastic relief at abandoning them both to bus tables at the Mad River Barn. Chick the Tree God, a Barn guest like myself, explained that he was three days late reporting back to work in Massachusetts but couldn't be held accountable—his truck was unable to drive south when it was snowing out.

And sure enough, it was snowing out. By some unexpected gift of nature, a cloud that belonged over Utah had stationed itself atop Mad River. The result was the lightest, driest, deepest snow that had fallen on the mountain in years. By nine o'clock, everyone was heading off to bed; tomorrow was going to be another powder day. If I wanted to hit the bars, I was told to drive into Waitsfield and drink with the "tourons" staying at Sugarbush, a resort a few miles down the road that is derisively referred to by Mad River regulars as Mascara Mountain. If I wanted to be a Mad River madman, I was advised to get some sleep and be at the hill by 6:40 A.M. for Milk Run.

♦ ♦ ♦

It was just before dawn and no longer snowing when I drove into Mad River's parking area, which is actually a crook in a hairpin turn on Route 17. Across the road, past a small cluster of base buildings, Mad River erupts. There is really no other way to describe it. From the valley floor to the rounded, 3,600-foot summit, General Stark Mountain does not pause to take a breath. There's no such thing as a flat spot at Mad River. Terrain served by the single chair, which chugs straight up the fall line, may very well have the longest continuous stretch of steepness anywhere in the United States, East Coast or West.

I crossed the street and saw that the chair was about to start up. Milk Run is a 40-year-old Mad River tradition: The first 25 people who show up when the ski patrol performs its early-morning mountain inspection are allowed to ride the single. The only stipulation is that if even one chair is skipped, Milk Run is over and the dillydallier and everyone behind him or her are not allowed on. The day I was there, only nine other skiers and one dog, a mutt named Cleo, arrived in time to board the chair.

As I passed over the first few lift towers—scaffolding-like structures that look like miniature Eiffel Towers—the earliest rays of morning washed over the mountain, illuminating the tips of snow-heavy firs. The chairlift is slow and arthritic, emitting an anemic pop each time a chair winds its way around the ancient bullwheel. At maximum capacity the lift hauls 400 people per hour. I had plenty of time to study the mountain on the 20-minute ride to the top.

Mad River is divided into two sections: the single-chair runs and the double-chair runs. Trails off the single have calmly utilitarian names like Chute, Lift Line, Fall Line, and Glades. At Mad River, there's no need to make skiers feel undeservedly proud merely because they made it down a run with a grisly name. The single-chair runs, which twist down the mountain with drunken abandon, are the hardest slopes at Mad River. They are the hardest slopes in the East— Stowe's front four included. Hell, they are some of the toughest slopes in America. Not only are they steep, they are entirely unmaintained. Obstacles aren't marked; ice isn't covered; bumps aren't smoothed. This is fine when the snow is soft and forgiving, as it was when I was there, but horrid during drought seasons. Snowmaking covers but eight acres of Mad River's 800-acre playground; groomers don't cover much more.

The Sunnyside double, rising at a 45-degree angle to the single (to the right if you're facing the mountain), services slightly easier runs. But only slightly; mostly they're just shorter. Basically, Mad River is for expert skiers. Nearly half of the 32 slopes acknowledged on the trail map are given a diamond; the dozens of off-the-map glades and rock jumps and narrow tree shots are all strictly in the double-diamond realm. Even intermediate trails at Mad River would easily earn expert status at most other Eastern areas—if they were open at all. Beginners and lower intermediates would be far happier at Mascara Mountain.

At a quarter to seven in the morning, of course, Mascara isn't open. A tradition like Milk Run—a veritable petri dish for lawsuits—could only take place at an area like Mad River. Once you've boarded the chair, Milk Run doesn't have any rules. You can ski any run you want, even one that'll be closed during regular hours. I hooked up with two locals I'd met at the Barn and we headed down Antelope, one of Mad River's expert-even-though-it's-marked-intermediate slopes. Basically, Antelope is endless bumps. But because nearly everyone who skis Mad River is an absurdly smooth skier, the bumps were cursive and fluid, conducive to a steady rhythm and easy to absorb. And the three inches of new snow lent our skis a sweet buoyancy.

Three quarters of the way down we veered right, off the trail and through a thin opening in the woods. This, I was informed, is a run called 19th Hole. Like several well-known Mad River slopes, it's not on the trail map; everyone who needs to know where it is already knows, and everyone who doesn't know shouldn't know. We flew down it at top speed—19th is an abandoned logging road—and were spit out, conveniently, at the back door of the Mad River Barn, more than a mile from the base of the single chair. Breakfast was a tall stack of blueberry pancakes.

♦ ♦ ♦

At nine o'clock I caught a ride back to the area for its official opening, then rode the single all day, rarely waiting in line for more than a minute. The lift began operating the same day Mad River did—December 11, 1948—and still runs primarily on original parts. The single chair creates an interesting skiing dynamic: Nobody has partners at Mad River Glen. Instead, you sort of slide from one group to another, with a solo run or two between, never remaining with the same people for more than an hour. Everyone seems to know one another at Mad River—the area sells about 700 season passes annually, and these people make up the vast majority of the daily skiers—so locals easily group and regroup, square-dance style. Even with the small handful people I knew from the Barn party, I didn't have to wait longer than a few minutes for a temporary partner. And each time I grouped up, I'd meet a few more locals.

My first mission was to ski Chute, the nasty bump run beneath the single. From the chair, Chute looks like a plaster cast of gale-force seas. It is home turf to Mad River's bump rippers, who show off for the audience above. And the seats are front row: The chair is so low to the ground it seems as though you could hook a skier's pompom with a dip of your ski tip. I skied Chute terribly, daunted by the locals' prowess and psyched out by the lift riders. So I immediately went back and tackled it again. I felt clumsy—Chute's intimidating steepness and vertebrae-straining bumps keep you perpetually off balance—but I did hear a "Sweet turns!" from a chair rider and so considered it a victory.

I skied every on-the-map single-chair run: Fall Line, as steep and bumped as Chute but with creatively whimsical gladed patches; Catamount, one-skier-at-a-time-narrow and enthrallingly turny; Grand Canyon, wide-open wall-to-wall bumps; Glades, kamikaze shots through tight trees; and Lynx, my favorite, a grove of neatly spaced white birches. All had remarkably distinct personalities—a concept that seems to have been left out of the equation in new computer-designed ski areas. And all were impossible to ski well the first time.

By the end of the day I was ragged. It was clear why everyone goes to sleep at nine. But I boarded the single a final time, just as snow started spilling down again and the thermometer headed south of zero. Tomorrow was going to be *another* powder day. I was shivering by the time I was greeted at the summit by George, the top operator, who was wrapped head-to-toe in a brown Carhartt one-piece. George presented me with a gap-toothed grin and said, "It's supposed to get much warmer," then paused, rubbing his midriff before adding the punchline: "In Florida."

That evening, I ate dinner at the Barn with Betsy Pratt. She is one of the most stubborn, most opinionated, most exasperating, most in-love-with-the-mountains people I have ever met. How many other ski-area owners actually *encourage* their skiers to get off marked runs and play in the woods? In one breath she'll quote Chief Seattle on environmentalism;

in another she'll bad-mouth Vermont's governor, Howard Dean. Between, she puffs on her pipe. A concise description of her came from one long-time local: "She's tweaked." She has worn the same navy-blue parka since time immemorial and can be seen on the slopes nearly every day. Pratt skis her area smooth and slow and in sync with everything around her, like the frontman in a blues ensemble. She is 66 years old and has lorded over the mountain since her husband, Trux, died in 1975. And make no mistake: Mad River is Betsy's mountain, through and through. What she says goes, and Pratt has never been one to bite her tongue.

On snowboarding: "Snowboarding on a ski mountain is like playing croquet on the 18th green—you can do it, but I don't think it's appropriate." (Snowboarding is forbidden at Mad River, and Pratt loves to tell about the time she sent away Governor Dean when he showed up at her area with a board.)

On snowmaking: "I hate man-made snow. If you want snowmaking, go ski somewhere else."

On ski-industry profiteering: "It doesn't make sense. You don't ask your rivers and lakes to make money; why ask your mountains?"

On why she's no longer a member of the Vermont Ski Areas Association: "They lie too much."

On Mad River's out-of-date facilities: "They're not that old. The Brooklyn Bridge was built in 1880 and people still use that."

On mainstream resorts: "Boring."

The tragic thing is that Betsy is thinking about retiring. Though she's been threatening this for the past decade, there are signs she's now serious. After 45 years of incorrigible unhipness, Mad River may soon be forced to acknowledge modern realities.

◆ ◆ ◆

I figured I should take advantage of Pratt's permissiveness while I still could. So the next morning I got on line for the single in order to ski Paradise, Mad River's most infamous run. Even referring to Paradise as a ski run seems deficient; it's too steeped in Mad River lore to be anything as humdrum as a ski run. Paradise is more a *concept*—an entire hillside of wooded backcountry with myriad skiing options. It was cut decades ago, not by the owners of Mad River, but by the skiers, and Paradise still does not appear on the trail map. It has, however, finally earned a mention in Mad River's brochure, along with this warning: "Until you become familiar with the area, you must ski with someone who understands Paradise and how to survive it." It says it right in the brochure: Paradise must be *understood.*

I had first heard of Paradise when I was very young. It was mentioned by other skiers with reverence—a run on Paradise is a visit to skiing's Oval Office, etc., etc.—yet spoken about only infrequently, preserving its cultish mystique. People referred to the run's waterfall jump as if it were a beast from Greek mythology. *It'll kill you. Fall and you die. You can't even look at it.* Paradise is the type of run more people talk about than actually attempt. Of course, I was itching to ski it. So I persuaded Eric the Deadhead, Kyle the Stockbroker, and Chick the Tree God to take me.

We gathered on the deck of the summit's decrepit warming hut, a prime spot for viewing the Green Mountains. The mountains are mogul-shaped and evergreen-blanketed—less severe and more serene than West Coast peaks—with a distinct rime line snaking its way across. We herringboned up a short hill and onto a path that led to Fall Line. A quick patch of easy bumps and we swung left, through an unmarked but well-tracked opening in the woods, and poled through trees so tightly packed only tiny beads of light made it to the snowy floor. I removed my sunglasses. And then, nailed to a birch in a small clearing, we saw a hand-painted wooden sign:

DANCER

WILDERNESS AREA • DO NOT SKI ALONE

CONDITIONS VARY GREATLY

NONCONVENTIONAL TERRAIN

HAZARDS MAY EXIST • NOT PATROLLED

We looked down a trail about the width of a catwalk. Eric, Kyle, and Chick leapt in. They banged knowingly through a collection of moguls, many with a rock surprise on the downhill face, then stopped and waited for me to catch up. It was time to jump the waterfall. The thing is indeed mean-looking:

a jagged agglomeration of rock one story high, encased in a foot-thick layer of jaundiced ice. It stretches the entire way across Paradise—a natural tollbooth of sorts. The landing zone is populated with white birches and choppy bumps, and is about as steep as anything you can descend without using a rope. This is not a place you want to fall.

My partners, obvious Paradise veterans, made the jump look simple. I'm a solid skier but no air maestro, so I eased over to a corner of the fall, a spot that looked the least dangerous to jump. After a minute of failed visualization, I decided to simply go for it. The snow was tracked but still soft, so a slight mishap wouldn't necessarily spell disaster. I pushed off, and felt that panicked tightening of all my muscles from throat to stomach as it dawned on me: *I'm flying.* I banked my skis to set up for a clean landing—one that wasn't going to send me into the trees—and thudded to earth. Beautiful, no, but at least upright. I was in.

My giddiness at successfully pulling off the jump emboldened me. I threw myself into the steep bumps at full speed, caution to the wind, the way Paradise should be skied—a whirling jig through bull-size moguls, over rock outcroppings and tree stumps and even a bale of hay. The powder between the bumps created geysers of spraying snow. I made a good 50 turns, all short, clipped half-moons, before flopping into a snowbank, legs burning.

The best was still to come. We ventured deep into the forest on a mission for untracked lines—Paradise has a thousand different options. On Paradise, however, you don't really ski trees; you ski *woods*. We each found an uncut swath, and silently went through the pre-tree-skiing ritual. Pole straps off. Goggles on. Mind ready to absorb the flood of a billion bits of bark-covered data all flying in your face at once.

I plunged in, hands in front of me like a ski racer, swatting low-lying brush out of the way. I bobbed and weaved, ski tips inches from tree trunks, shoulders skimming against bark. Branches cracked like bull whips, smacking goggles, tinging pole shafts, clawing pants. Ski tails connecting with wood produced jarring bass-drum *thwonks*. Snow tumbled from treetops. I picked up speed, with no place wide enough to check it; faster, faster, dizzy from the kaleidoscope of shadow and light, faster, bloody-lipped from branch burn, faster, a gruesome crash moments away, seconds, milliseconds, faster, then out of nowhere, an opening—*stop!*

We skied four pitches like this, through all of lower Paradise. And then, literally inches from liberation, I crashed. On the final pitch, I could see the light of the catwalk marking Paradise's end, and decided to straight-run the last section. It didn't work. I finished the run with a pair of shredded ski pants and a good round of ribbing from my group.

After skiing that day I drove into Waitsfield seeking Marsha Nicholson, proprietor of The Village Seamstress. Marsha looked at my ski pants, then asked if I was newly arrived in the area.

I said I was.

She asked if I had been tree skiing when I ripped my pants.

I admitted I had.

"Welcome to Mad River," she said, and began sewing.

Six Feet Under

Minute one: Within seconds, I knew I had made a poor decision. "Put your hands in front of your face and create a breathing space," instructed Bill Lerch, the owner of Gallatin Search Dogs, just before he started piling snow on top of me. From my position, lying fetuslike in a six-foot-deep snow pit dug into a closed section of trail at Montana's Big Sky ski resort, Lerch looked like a shovel-wielding colossus. At least he did for a moment; then he threw a shovelful of snow over my head, and I shut my eyes.

I tried to tell him to wait, to stop for a moment so we could reconsider this whole plan, but my murmurings of protest were lost beneath the snow. Whether I wanted to be or not, I was a volunteer avalanche victim, a participant in the training of a search-and-rescue dog. A skillful avalanche dog, Lerch had informed me, can perform the work of 25 human ground searchers. This advantage is potentially lifesaving. According to the Colorado Avalanche Information Center, less than half of all avalanche victims recovered after 30 minutes beneath the snow are found alive. And as the number of avalanche deaths in the United States has repeatedly surpassed its all-time high in recent winters, there has been a commensurate upsurge in the demand for rescue dogs. Big Sky keeps three of Lerch's dogs on full-time duty. It takes about a year to train them, Lerch told me, but to stay sharp, they need constant practice. I could help save a skier's life simply by agreeing to be buried by Lerch and dug up by Yeti, a long-haired German shepherd who was barking his head off about 200 feet down the slope. Ten minutes, he said, was all it would take.

Minute two: The first thing that struck me was the weight. All those odes and reveries and snappy marketing logos about snow's divine fluffiness have failed to consider a person stuck six feet under the stuff. It turns out that snow, even the most buoyant powder, is actually heavy. So heavy, in fact, that it rendered me completely unable to move. The snow upon my chest lay with such force that breathing could only be accomplished through brief, staccato gasps. I considered calling for help—in my left hand, shoved a few inches from my face, was a walkie-talkie to be used in case of emergency. But the embarrassment of ruining the training overrode my fear of lapsing into absolute panic. I decided to lay longer. How much longer, I wasn't sure. The only way I could mark the passage of time was to substitute my clipped breaths for the ticks of a clock's second hand.

Minute three: Another serious miscalculation was the amount of light I thought I'd receive. I figured six feet of snow would be similar to six feet of water—I'd be in the dark, but at least able to see a pale glow emanating from the surface. Maybe the experience would even be downright ethereal, the snow pit awash with luminescence. Not so, I soon discovered. Once I resigned myself to the snow's immense weight, I opened my eyes and blinked a few times. The difference between open and shut was nil—I was compacted in a vat of absolute black. I strained my eyes for something to focus on, any sliver of light, and failing in this, I became dizzy. All conception of what was up or down vanished.

Minute four: With sight denied, hearing took over. I had expected to experience transcendent silence, but reality, once again, presented an unfortunate surprise. As the snow settled around me, seemingly upset at my intrusion, it created noises like the cracking of wet wood in a campfire. And when my body heat warmed the pit, the sounds intensified, metamorphosing into protracted sloshes, like hunger cries from an empty stomach.

Minute five: It was the sound of my own breathing, however, that was most disturbing. My hole was an echo chamber, one that protracted and amplified every nuance of my gasping breaths. Inhalation sounded like screeching brakes; exhalation like a foghorn. They were startling sounds, ones that seemed not to come from my body but instead to creep out of the darkness, as if I were listening to my own voice on a garbled recording.

Minute six: Deep layers of snow, I found out the hard way, become compacted into brick-size, sharp-edged chunks. These jabbed into me like a bed of nails, stinging through my ski clothes in all places at once. There was one spot, however, that felt worse than the rest. An especially sharp chunk was lodged beneath my right calf, poking into the muscle. Soon it started to itch. Then it began to really itch. And then it became what must certainly be the most torturous itch in recorded history, a burning, crawling, life-is-not-worth-living-like-this itch. Moving my hand down to scratch it was impossible, as was wiggling my leg away from its source. I tried anyway, of course, straining as a person might struggle against a straitjacket, becoming agitated and sweaty and eventually enraged, all the while accomplishing precisely nothing. At that moment, I believe I would've exchanged a year's salary for the opportunity to make one scratch. I grabbed my radio and called for help.

Minute seven: The sweat produced from my struggles did not mix well with the snowy surroundings. A chill started at the tips of my toes, and swiftly washed over my body, producing a violent shivering that cramped my muscles. My fingers were the worst. Even with gloves on, they became numb and nearly functionless. I realized that my calling into the radio was for naught. The walkie-talkie was in an awkward position, and with my frozen fingers I was unable to hold down the talk button for more than an instant. For all Lerch knew, I was sitting in my snow cell humming love songs.

Minute eight: Panic is the human body's version of an avalanche. The various strata of fear—anxiety, dread, anguish, horror—build up like separate snowfalls, each one gradually eroding your resolve until one moment, usually without warning, all the defense mechanisms (rationalization, prayer, blind hope) topple, and raw emotion rushes out. I was near my breaking point, pushing helplessly against the sides of my pit, choking on the stale air, shivering, blind, immobile, waiting for the moment of panic to strike.

Minute nine: In the end, though, I managed to hold myself together. I started speaking aloud, repeating what Lerch had said earlier: This was a controlled situation, no danger at all, a safe practice session, 10 minutes, 10 minutes, 10 minutes. There was no way anything truly dangerous could happen to me. Were this a real avalanche . . . the thought was too terrible to complete. Instead, the rules for survival flashed through my head like a mantra: Swim to the top, try and grab a tree or a rock, thrust a hand or foot to the surface, create an air pocket, wait and don't panic, wait and don't panic, wait, wait, wait. But with my distorted perception of time, I was positive 10 minutes had long since passed. I had waited long enough, I decided, longer than long enough. I summoned all my strength and clutched the walkie-talkie. I heard the talk button click, opening the channels. And I begged for freedom.

Minute ten: As I begged, I heard a different sound. It was a hollow crunching noise, almost like footfalls, only they were not exactly footfalls but a sort of spasmodic scratching, as if someone right near me in the snow was in a full-bore panic. I was baffled for a moment, and then I heard barking, and everything happened in a rush. There was a crack of light, the furry tip of a paw, a blur of furiously churning paws, an opening, and then blue, blue skies, the bluest anything could ever be. And the instant I could move, I lifted my hands to embrace the blue and received a warm, wet lick across my face.

The Run of a Lifetime

O n the side of a snowy road in a country where evidence of
skiing dates back more than 4,000 years, I waited to take
an extraordinary run. It was a few minutes past sunrise on
February 9, three days before the start of the Lillehammer
Olympics, and I had just been dropped off by a van on a
deserted side street in southeastern Norway. At the road's
edge, stuck into a four-foot-high snowbank, was a small
wooden sign that read, simply, LEG 28. This is where I was supposed to stand and wait my turn to run with the Olympic
torch.

I was wearing the official torchbearer's uniform: white
polyester wind jacket, white polyester rain pants, white ski
hat, white mittens, white running shoes. I looked as if I were

about to report to work at the generic-food aisle of the local supermarket. The outfit probably would have made me feel silly were it not for the fact that everyone else in the van— the people running legs 29, 30, and 31—was wearing exactly the same garb. Also, I knew that just about everyone in Norway would have traded their finest reindeer-skin rug for the opportunity to slip on the generic jogging suit and carry the Olympic torch for a few minutes. More than 100,000 applications were sent to the Lillehammer Olympic Organizing Committee for a spot on the relay; only 7,500 people were selected by lottery to participate in the 75-day, 5,000-mile lap around Norway.

Originally I had planned to explore the "cradle of skiing," as historians often call Norway, by actually skiing. I'd wanted to telemark in the province of Telemark, make christie turns in Christiania, and then travel north to the town of Rodoy and view prehistoric cave paintings of skiers, the sport's oldest known documentation. Finally, I was going to celebrate in the southern hamlet of Ski—the only town in the world with such a name, at least according to the Norwegian tourist board.

But nothing worked out. I had accepted a job as a researcher for the Olympic staff of CBS television, and I learned the hard way that the workload—15 hours a day, seven days a week—left scarcely enough time to sleep, let alone travel or ski. I had dragged my boards halfway around the globe only to see them propped in a corner of my cubicle, where they mocked me daily for abandoning the relative bacchanal of magazine writing for the big-bucks world of TV.

It was while researching a television piece a few days before the start of the Games, however, that I became fascinated by the torch relay. The flame, I learned, was first ignited outside the home of Sondre Nordheim, the 19th-century ski pioneer and inventor of the first binding to firmly secure the boot to the ski. It then traveled through every Norwegian county, being carried at times by people on cross-country skis, in wheelchairs, on horseback, in kayaks, on reindeer-drawn sleds, and, more than once, by swimmers backstroking across a fjord. It was helicoptered to an oil platform in the North Sea and flown to the frozen islands of Svalbard, where it was run through some of the northernmost communities in the world. The torch was carried through blinding blizzards and minus-40-degree temperatures and perpetual winter darkness. With the relay still a few days from completion, more than half of the country's 4.3 million people had watched the torch pass by, and 2,500 towns had hosted special celebrations to commemorate its arrival. This was the most ambitious torch run in Winter Olympic history.

If I didn't have time to ski, I realized I could at least tap into the Olympic spirit by participating in the relay. I convinced my bosses at CBS that an on-site investigation of the relay was essential, but Olympic Committee underlings informed me that there were absolutely no running slots available. So I took my case to the top. I tracked down the torch relay's project manager, Eivind Rossen, and presented a half dozen maudlin reasons why I should be allowed to run. I pleaded, and, in all likelihood, crossed the line into groveling. Rossen said there might *possibly* be a slot available.

And then I mentioned pins. If you have never been to an Olympics, you can not possibly fathom the importance of commemorative pins. Every company affiliated with the Olympics produces a special pin, and during the Games these badges are like gold, only more valuable. If you can get hold of a decent enough supply of them, you will come as close as you'll ever get on this planet to omnipotence. The timely presentation of an Olympic pin can unlock doors, cause security guards to look the other way, or give you a double shot at the bar for the price of a single. (Nevermind that the pins are virtually worthless once the Games are over.) When I told Rossen I had access to a sizcable cache of CBS pins, he suddenly remembered there being an unfilled relay slot early the next morning.

I awoke in the middle of the night and caught a bus to the town of Elverum, site of the day's relay headquarters. (The torch was run about 12 hours daily then kept lit but immobile overnight.) I gave away every CBS pin I owned and several I didn't own, and was handed my white runner's outfit. Then the van came by and brought me to my designated spot, an evergreen-lined road in the midst of rolling farmlands, where I was told to wait for the flame.

Fifteen minutes later, through the dim morning light, I saw the top of the flame as it appeared over the crest of a small hill, bobbing like the pompom of a ski hat. Soon the whole torch was visible, and finally a white-suited runner. All I had to do to keep the relay intact was to move the torch 500 meters and pass it off to the next runner. If all went well, three days later it would arrive in Lillehammer's main stadium and, following a dramatic flight in the hand of a ski jumper, be used to ignite the Olympic cauldron during the opening ceremony. As the flame approached, I triple-tied my shoelaces, practiced running in place, and made a humble petition to the Deity of Clumsiness for protection from doing something horribly embarrassing, like dropping the torch or slipping on the ice or both.

The handoff was smooth. I clenched the torch's handle as I would a ski pole on a double-diamond run—in a death grip—and set off, taking slow, deliberate strides. The torch was exquisite: four feet long, the handle made from the white wood of a Norwegian fir, the top section made of silver. It curved gently, like an elephant's tusk, and weighed approximately 10 pounds. There were six wicks—five small ones running down the silver part of the shaft and a large one on top. With each gust of wind, the interplay of the flames created a new image. A headwind made it look like a gently waving flag; a heavy gust from behind caused the fire to dance wildly, shooting red and orange embers into the milky sky.

I ran with the torch held high and a figure skater's smile draped across my face. The road was closed so that I could run on it, as if I were some visiting head of state. The air swirled with snowflakes, the kind that fall slowly, like leaves, and glint in the sun. I ran by an elderly man who carried a cowbell in one hand and a Norwegian flag in the other; he gave me three sharp clangs as I jogged by.

A hundred meters farther, I passed an elementary school. Two dozen children stood alongside the road, their faces painted red and white, Norway's national colors. They had constructed a giant snowman in the schoolyard and had painted its face red and white, too. When the children saw me coming, they burst into an adorably off-key rendition of the Norwegian national anthem.

At the far end of the school, I saw another person dressed in white. It took a moment for me to realize that she was the next runner. I had been carrying the torch for all of three minutes and, except for a cramp in my shoulder, felt as if I could go on for hours, jogging on pure adrenaline. But when I reached the waiting runner, I had no choice but to hand the torch over. As the relay continued, I sat on the curb, catching my breath, and looked back where I had run. Pressed into the fresh snow, each so faint it looked more like a shadow, was a long string of footprints—some of the finest tracks I've ever laid.